Algeria of the Generals

Lyes Laribi

ALGERIA OF THE GENERALS

Max Milo Éditions
Collection Essais-Documents, Paris, 2023
www.maxmilo.com
ISBN : 978-2-31501-230-5

To my father.

PREFACE

In his first book, *Dans les Geôles de Nezzar (In Nezzar's Jails)*, Lyes Laribi, then a young trade unionist and peaceful student, gave us a direct account of what he had to suffer in his flesh and in his dignity as early as 1991, simply because he was politically committed, nurtured by the values of freedom, justice and emancipation, for himself, his neighborhood, his university and his country. No "normative" reason could justify his imprisonment. Neither a fundamentalist, as those who take the liberty of forcibly civilizing those who stand in their way say today; nor even a "moderate, politically correct" Islamist. He even called himself a democrat!

This young student will be locked up and physically and morally mutilated without having done anything reprehensible, but only because he had a conscience and principles. In truth, having a conscience and the courage to say what it dictates is experienced as an extreme danger by a regime that can only exist if it has a monopoly on thought and language. Unfortunately, he came to know the reality of the war being waged on the people, its barbaric practices and its madness, from different vantage points and angles: from his cell, through contact with jailers, political prisoners, common law prisoners, terrorists and visitors; from his home, in the heart of a working-class neighborhood, where he could experience the heartbreak of families and the complexity of real-life situations; through his encounters, fortuitous or otherwise, with those directly involved in this war. Liberated, he went into exile in Europe. For a long time without rights, he lived on the margins of society, experiencing fear and feeling hunted for a long time. A conscience is even more dangerous in the midst of the poor abroad, where it still has room to maneuver, than in Algeria, where comfort is strictly under surveillance.

Today, in *L'Algérie des Généraux*, he tells us very simply how he understands this war, this regime and this nightmare, which, alas, he shares with the majority of Algerians. And that's where the interest and importance of his testimony lie in understanding and taking a stand. This book is first and foremost a testimony to the war waged on the Algerian people in the 1990s by its police, army and political apparatchiks, who shied away from any kind of business dealings or adventurism. It is neither an analysis of a political regime, nor the work of a political activist.

The witness is in an exceptionally new position, rich in lessons for all those seeking information on how this war unfolded: he has directly observed in detail the internal links between terrorist leaders and military officers in charge of the political police, the division of tasks between this same police force and the most extremist of political fundamentalists, the collusion between totalitarianisms to enslave the people, terrorize them and prevent them for a long time from hoping.

The author gives us his experience without theorizing or even explaining, and this is what gives the book its merit and strength. At the same time, he attempts, through his own experience, to understand how the Algerian revolution came to be handed over to this type of practice and this type of man, in a war that officially left two hundred thousand dead and missing, as well as in a reconciliation without trial strictly reserved on both sides for the designers, decision-makers and executors of the dirty work, and finally in the peace granted with contempt to a humiliated people, suffering in silence. He finds the source of the evil in 1958, when the Algerians' struggle for independence was confiscated by the military stationed at the borders, framed by deserters from the colonial army, following the destruction of the political leadership living among the people. These deserters are still there; the author only indirectly suggests how these soldiers nevertheless gradually represented an authoritarian class power supported by the few bureaucratic elites of the time, and slowly evolving into a police and financial oligarchy.

But that's another story; his is the fascinating tale of real cops, real terrorists and terrorists on duty, real popular leaders and "radical" leaders on duty.

It's a first, and well worth the detour.

Ghazi Hidouci,
former political player in the attempt
democratization of institutions,
now in exile.

INTRODUCTION

Since Bouteflika's hospitalization in Val-de-Grâce in December 2005, following the worsening of an illness shrouded in great opacity, Algerians have once again been confronted with the spectres that populate El-Mouradia, the presidential palace. They know that their country is sick of its men.

Forty years after its hard-won independence, Algeria is still struggling to find its way. The political situation remains deadlocked. Democracy remains a pipe dream. Power has remained in the hands of two clans of generals - those of Liamine Zeroual and Khaled Nezzar - who have never stopped tearing each other apart.

As for the economy, it's at an impasse. Algeria remains dependent on oil revenues. Attempts at reform and liberalization are resisted by all those predatory clienteles grouped around a few high-profile individuals. Unemployment affects a large proportion of the working population (-17%

in 2005, according to the official version). The regression has been so considerable over the last decade that it led the United Nations Development Programme (UNDP) to classify Algeria as a priority country in its 2003 Human Development Report. In this list, the country occupies a lowly position, despite booming oil revenues.

Since Bendjeddid's resignation in 1992, Algeria has remained in a state of emergency. The security situation remains unclear, even if terrorist acts against civilians have declined.

The second Algerian war, a civil war, left 150,000 dead, hundreds of thousands orphaned, tens of thousands tortured, not to mention thousands missing.

Civil liberties continue to be trampled underfoot. The absence of civic representation has given rise to a riot culture in which conflicts are always settled by violence. Despair drives young people to suicide, and their only dream is to emigrate to faraway lands. Crisis follows crisis.

This book was requested by many readers of my first book, *Dans les geôles de Nezzar*[1]. In particular, I tried to provide factual answers to the following questions: What is the nature of the Algerian regime? Was the army in favor of the democratization process after the riots of October 1988? Why this second war, and who benefits from the continuing crisis? What are the ways out of this impasse?

---

1. Éditions Paris-Méditerranée, 2002.

Allow me finally to quote a key phrase. It comes from the mouth of the current President of the Republic, who, in a speech in September 2001, declared: "The State does not serve the nation but harms it." A word to the wise.

A large part of the book is devoted to the last decade; I've tried to look back at some of the major events that, I believe, had an impact on Algeria's future:

- the assassination of historical figures from the War of Independence, from Abane Ramdane to Mohamed Boudiaf;

- the many coups d'état that have punctuated the history of independent Algeria, starting with the one directed against the Provisional Government of the Algerian Republic (GPRA);

- certain criminal acts and economic decisions, which I'll describe in detail.

But above all, I've tried to understand how a few generals were able to control Algeria's destiny, and draw red lines around their legal showcases (presidents of the Republic, heads of government, ministers, judges, deputies...). How did this opaque, parallel power replace legal power? What links unite these men? How are civil and military clients organized around them? How are conflicts between these men settled? How can these clans be defeated and Algeria's future taken away from them? In short, how can we restore the voice, dignity and confidence of the Algerian people?

I

CONFISCATED INDEPENDENCE
(1962-1965)

Before turning to the period of Algerian independence, which began in July 1962, I'd like to look back at two events that took place during the war of liberation, and whose consequences were dramatic: the death of Abane Ramdane and the creation of the Ministry of Armament and General Liaison (MALG), the intelligence service of the National Liberation Front (FLN).

1. THE DEATH OF ABANE RAMDANE

The Algerian people, under French rule since 1830, rose up against the occupying power on November 1st, 1954. This armed uprising was the culmination of decades of revolts, attempts at compromise and failure. It was launched by a handful of men under the aegis of the FLN.

On November 1st, 1954, Abane Ramdane was in prison. He had been locked up in 1950 for his membership of the nationalist movement, which he had joined in 1946 after studying at the college in Blida, near Algiers. He was released in January 1955 and joined the ranks of the insurrection that had just broken out. He understood that this insurrection, to stay alive, must not remain in the hands of the CRUA. A congress would give the movement a national dimension. Along with Larbi Ben M'hidi, Abane Ramdane was the organizer of the Soummam Congress, held on August 20, 1956, which defined the boundaries between political and military power. He was the ideologist of the Algerian revolution. His assassination marked a decisive moment in the transformation of the Algerian state. He had a strong personality and a solid culture. A Jacobin, he was behind the rallying of all national political forces (except the Communist Party), including the religious forces represented by the "oulémas[2]" under the aegis of the FLN. He came into conflict with military leaders, believing that politics should take precedence over the military, and the interior over the exterior.

The arrest and subsequent execution of Larbi Ben M'hidi by Colonel Bigeard's paratroopers, the failure of the eight-day strike in Algiers in January 1957, the unan-

---

2. Ulama are the theologians of Islam.

nounced exile of the Comité de Coordination et d'Exécution (CCE) to Tunis in June 1957[3], shifting alliances and personal ambitions precipitated his downfall. At a meeting in Tunis[4], Colonel Boussouf, in charge of wilaya[5] V, and Boumediene, his deputy to whom he had delegated a large part of his powers, were particularly taken to task by Abane Ramdane, who criticized them for their behavior towards the civilian population in the areas under their control. This type of attitude was unfortunately repeated with certain other warlords, whom he never failed to castigate publicly. His authority is such that no one dares confront him openly. One day, when receiving several senior officials, he flew into a violent rage, threatening to denounce them publicly: "Then I'll go back to Algeria, to lead the struggle among the maquisards and militants." This led Krim Belkacem, regarded as the head of the army since the Soummam Congress, to react at the meeting of August 27, 1957, shouting to Abane Ramdane: "Who started the war? Who suffered the most? A majority is emerging in favor of the colonels, whether you like it or not[6]."

Abane Ramdane was dropped at the last moment by those closest to him. The first political crime was then organized by the three "B"s: Belkacem Krim, Boussouf Abdelhafid

---

3. Following the repression suffered after the eight-day strike and the setting up of a cell to track down FLN leaders, the CCE decided to go into exile abroad.
4. Pierre Miquel, *La Guerre d'Algérie*, Fayard, 1993, p. 325.
5. There are 48 wilayas in Algeria.
6. Pierre Miquel, *op. cit.* p. 325.

and Bentobbal Lakhdar (head of Wilaya II): Belkacem Krim, Boussouf Abdelhafid and Bentobbal Lakhdar (head of Wilaya II). Abane Ramdane was lured into an ambush. Messages from FLN liaison services began to arrive from Morocco, reporting militants arrested and sequestered, and stocks of weapons seized by Moroccan authorities. The messages became increasingly alarming, and King Mohamed V showed himself willing to discuss them and find a solution, but only with the FLN's main leader, Abane Ramdane. The latter was persuaded by the three main instigators: Belkacem, Boussouf and Bentobbal. Belkacem went to Morocco to prepare for his companion's arrival. A few days later, Abane Ramdane, accompanied by Krim Belkacem and Mahmoud Cherif, both members of the CCE, arrived in Morocco via Spain. They were met by Boussouf at the airfield. Abane Ramdane was taken to an isolated farmhouse. As soon as he arrived, six men pounced on him and tied him up, while one of them squeezed his Adam's apple with his wrist. He was taken into an adjoining room and strangled. He was thus assassinated on December 27, 1957 in Morocco by the men of Colonel Boussouf, creator of the MALG[7].

---

7. Before becoming the "Ministère de l'Armement et des Liaisons Générales", the MALG was the Direction Centrale des Liaisons Générales (DCLG), then the Ministère des Liaisons Générales et des Communications (MLGC).

A few months later, in May 1958, *El Moudjahid,* the FLN newspaper, paid tribute[8] to this courageous man, who is said to have succumbed to his wounds sustained during a skirmish with the enemy: the first lie about a political assassination in a press organization had just been told. This method was considered to be the best way of thwarting any political opposition to the regime, and is, unfortunately, still valid today.

The assassination of Abane Ramdane, accused of authoritarianism and even treason by his fellow soldiers, marked the effective seizure of power by the military, who would never relinquish it. The Algerian revolution gave birth to a dictatorship: a militarized political system was put in place, using every means to ensure its survival.

2. SETTING UP THE INFERNAL MACHINE AND THE MILITARY SEIZURE OF POWER

Colonel Boussouf, in charge of Wilaya V, one of the main conspirators against Abane Ramdane and directly responsible for his death, was the creator of the MALG, the forerunner of military security during the War of Independence. The MALG was based in Tripoli, Libya. A cadre school, run by Khalifa, father of former *golden boy*

---

8. Khalifa Mameri, *Abane Ramdane, héros de la guerre d'Algérie*, L'Harmattan, 1988, p. 301.

Rafik Khalifa, was created, from which the future heads of military security, known as the *"Boussouf boys"*, would emerge. In 1962, just before his dismissal, Colonel Boussouf decided to send his students to learn the practices of the KGB[9] in the latter's schools, under the famous "Red Carpet" code[10]. The *"Boussouf boys"* learned a wide range of methods for eliminating opponents, but above all they were initiated into the art of apparatus terrorism. Their apprenticeship was more than just a support, which Boumediene and his future successors were to benefit from after independence.

Military Security (MS), currently the Intelligence and Surveillance Directorate (DRS), is the regime's political police force. It represents the backbone of the regime, and has ensured and continues to ensure its survival. It is a veritable institution that weaves its web everywhere. The army, ministries, embassies, state-owned companies, local authorities, universities, political parties, associations and the public and private press will all be infiltrated and, where necessary, manipulated. No man can hold on to power without his support. It's a state within a state. Rafik Khalifa's rapid growth in the 1990s illustrates the power of the network formed by former MALG members.

1958 was marked above all by the announcement, on September 19, of the creation of the GPRA, with Ferhat Abbas, a pharmacist by profession and a seasoned politician, as its president. He had been in charge of the Union

---

9. Secret services of the former USSR.
10. Reporters sans frontières, *Le Drame algérien*, La Découverte, 1994, p. 90.

Démocratique du Manifeste Algérien (UDMA) party before joining the FLN in April 1955 (he had been arrested in the aftermath of the insurrection and had just been released). Ferhat Abbas remained at its head until the 4th Congress of the CNRA, held in Tripoli from August 5 to 22, 1961, when he was deposed and replaced by Youcef Benkhada, another pharmacist and centralist member of the nationalist movement since 1943.

According to the official version, this change in the GPRA's leadership was tactical and consisted of a softening that led to the Evian agreements with the French state. But the reality is as follows: Krim Belkacem, who was increasingly suspicious of Boumediene, who had meanwhile become Chief of Staff, encouraged this change, which he saw as strategic. This explains the GPRA's public disavowal of the Boumediene staff and commanders Ali Mendjeli and Kaid Ahmed. Colonel Boumediene, whose real name was Mohamed Boukharouba, was born on August 23, 1932 in a village near the town of Guelma in eastern Algeria. He joined the nationalist movement in 1949. He studied in Constantine, then in Tunis, and finally at El-Azhar University in Cairo. He took command of Wilaya V in 1957, then of the Oujda headquarters in Morocco. He then took over operational command of the West, before becoming Chief of Staff of the Armée de Libération Nationale (ALN). It was then that Boumediene forged the spirit of submission to authority, and above all built up an authoritarian administration favored by the presence of civil servants.

On March 19, 1962, after several unsuccessful meetings, a ceasefire was signed between the French government and the head of the GPRA delegation, Krim Belkacem: these were the "Evian Accords", which would lead, on July 3, 1962, to a popular referendum proclaiming Algeria's independence. But as independence approached, the struggle for power raged between yesterday's companions: on one side, the GPRA, and on the other, the Oujda clan[11], i.e. the army staff, backed by the MALG services.

The confrontation between the two parties took place in Tripoli during the congress of the National Council of the Algerian Revolution (CNRA), between May 27 and June 7, 1962: the "OAS affair[12]" (Secret Army Organization). The divorce was consummated.

The GPRA returned to Algiers on July 1st, 1962. On July 11th, Colonel Boumediene's staff moved to Tlemcen with Ahmed Ben Bella and Mohamed Khider.

Ben Bella was born on December 25, 1916 in Maghnia, of Moroccan peasant parents who had emigrated to the Algerian-Moroccan border. He joined the nationalist movement in 1947. He was arrested in 1950 and sentenced two years later to seven years in prison. He escaped in 1952 and joined Hocine Ait Ahmed and Mohamed Khider in Cairo, with whom he later formed the FLN's external

---

11. In reference to the Moroccan town on the border with western Algeria, where the headquarters' rear base is located.
12. Gilbert Meynier, *Histoire intérieure du FLN (1954-1962)*, Fayard, 2002, p. 638.

delegation. He was arrested a second time in 1956, following the hijacking of his plane from Morocco to Tunis, along with Hocine Ait Ahmed, Mohamed Khider, Mohamed Boudiaf and Mostefa Lacheref. He was incarcerated in the Santé prison and released in 1962. He then joined forces with Colonel Boumediene to seize power. On July 22, he proclaimed a political bureau in front of Mohamed Khider, Ferhat Abbas, Colonel Boumediene and his entire staff.

On July 27, Ait Ahmed, one of the historic leaders of the Algerian revolution and former head of the armed wing of the PPA-MTLD (secret organization), who had played a leading role in the insurrection against France in 1954 by helping to found the FLN, and who had defended the Algerian cause before the United Nations, resigned from the government. The border army went on the offensive: clashes broke out at the gates of Algiers. Thousands were killed. The maquisards of the interior were swept aside by a better-equipped, better-organized, more rested army, which had integrated into its ranks all deserters from the French army.

France threatened to intervene. The population took to the streets. From all this tragedy, we shall remember Mohamed Boudiaf's famous phrase: "The coup d'état, if by any chance it were to succeed, would mean the establishment of a fascist dictatorship."

The crisis thus turned to the advantage of the Oujda clan, which relied on the border army to seize power.

3. Insurrection in Kabylia

At a time when the dissensions within the nationalist movement caused by the struggle for power were in full swing, the people initially let their joy explode. Magnificent demonstrations were organized in all Algerian towns and villages to celebrate the independence they had won, at a heavy price in terms of death and suffering. But a few days later, the people were faced with a merciless war between their own leaders, who wanted to share the spoils. And so, all those women, children, men and old people who had taken to the streets chanting *"Tahya djazâir[13]!"*, demonstrated once again, but this time under cries of *"Sebaa snine barakat[14]"*. This second descent of the people into the streets precipitated the fall of the GPRA and the accession of the Oujda clan to power.

On September 20, 1962, a Constituent Assembly was elected. It invested the government of Ahmed Ben Bella, who himself became President of the Council. The members of the Oujda clan then shared out the positions of responsibility, with the exception of Colonel Boussouf[15], who, in August 1962, was dismissed by the Boumediene-Ben Bella couple and their men. This first government included all those who had taken part in the July 20, 1962 meeting in Oran, but no member of the

---

13. "Vive l'Algérie!"
14. "Seven years is enough."
15. Reporters sans frontières, *op. cit.* p. 90.

last GPRA. Thus, Ahmed Ben Bella became President, Houari Boumediene Minister of Defense, Mohamed Khider Secretary General of the FLN, and Ferhat Abbas President of the National Assembly. In the eyes of Colonel Boumediene and his famous "*boys*", this division was only temporary, allowing the storm to pass.

A few months later, Colonel Boumediene assumed the vice-presidency of the Council. Mohamed Khider quickly understood his strategy and asked Ahmed Ben Bella to return the army to the barracks. When Ben Bella refused, Mohamed Khider decided to resign as Secretary General of the FLN on April 16, 1963. He may have thought that his resignation would make Ahmed Ben Bella realize how dangerous his Minister of Defense, who was also Vice-President of the Council, was. But seeing that he was incapable of understanding things, he decided to go into exile.

In 1964, in Geneva, he made a remarkable statement condemning the policies pursued by the authorities in Algiers. Of course, in the meantime, the propaganda machine had tried to smear him, calling him a thief and accusing him of embezzling the FLN treasury[16] - an accusation without any foundation, since his wife returned it just after his death. According to those close to him, Mohamed Khider considered that this money belonged to the Algerian people, and he wanted to use it as part of a government in

---

16. The sum was 5,751,844,638 old francs (see Gilbert Meynier, *op. cit.*).

exile whose mission would be to overthrow the government in Algiers and get rid of Colonel Boumediene. But his thoughts and wishes were in vain, and his plans remained in the preparatory stage, as a criminal hand took his life: he was assassinated on January 4, 1967 in Madrid by a certain Youcef Dakhmouche, a mobster and gold trafficker between Morocco and Algeria.

The delinquent, who was serving a prison sentence, was offered a contract to kill in exchange for his release, and he accepted. The investigation carried out by the Spanish police revealed the role played by the Algerian embassy in Madrid and by a certain Boukhalfa, the cultural attaché, in the elimination of Mohamed Khider.

A few weeks after the latter's resignation, the security services had dismantled the Parti de la Révolution Socialiste (PRS) and arrested its main leaders, including its leader, Mohamed Boudiaf (who had created the PRS on September 27, 1962), one of the founding members of the FLN and an early nationalist militant: he was arrested on June 21, 1963 at the Hydra bridge by agents of the Sécurité Militaire, then transferred to Tsabit, in Algeria's far south. After five months of arbitrary detention, he was released and forced into exile.

A few days earlier, on June 9, 1963, Hocine Ait Ahmed had delivered a violent indictment of Ahmed Ben Bella and his policies. On September 29, he announced the creation of the Front des Forces Socialistes (FFS).

On October 10, during the Sable War[17], the government declared general mobilization and went on the offensive in Kabylia. The Armée Nationale Populaire (ANP) opened fire on troops in the seventh region of Kabylia. Ait Ahmed and Colonel Mohand Oulhadj went underground with their supporters, but on November 12, an agreement was reached between Ben Bella and Commandant Mohand (or El Hadj). Ait Ahmed continued the resistance. He was arrested on October 17, 1964, sentenced to death and later pardoned. He escaped from El-Harrach prison in 1966 and went into exile.

Another armed revolt broke out in 1964 under the command of Colonel Chaabani, supported by Mohamed Khider, and was put down in bloodshed. Colonel Chaabani was arrested, tried by a military court, sentenced to death and executed. At this trial, the public prosecutor was a certain Captain Chadli Bendjeddid, future President of the Republic. On August 14, 1963, Ferhat Abbas resigned as head of the National Assembly in a bid to distance himself from the FLN's constitutional project. He was arrested on July 3, 1964, at his home in Kouba, and held incommunicado at El-Biar in a disused clinic until October 30, along with his companions in misfortune: Abderrahmane Farès, former president of the provisional executive, Amar Bentoumi, former Minister of Justice, Commandant Azzeddine, Commandant Larbi Berredjem, deputies

---

17. Border dispute between Algeria and Morocco.

Boualem Oussedik and Brahim Mezhoudi, Ait Chaalal, future ambassador to Brussels, and others. Ferhat Abbas was deported to Bechar, in the south-west of France, and was not released until June 8, 1965.

4. The coup d'état of June 19, 1965

On August 28, 1963, the Algerian Parliament "adopted" a Constitution. Drafted at the Majestic[18], a cinema in Algiers, by a group close to Ahmed Ben Bella, it was to be imposed on Parliament instead. This provoked the resignation and ire of a number of key players in the Algerian revolution, including parliamentary president Ferhat Abbas. It was ratified by a pseudo-referendum held on September 8, 1963. As a result, Ahmed Ben Bella became President of the Republic on September 15, 1963. With this legitimacy from the ballot box, he set about implementing his socialist program, based on self-management of commercial and industrial enterprises.

But Ahmed Ben Bella was wary of Boumediene, thanks to whom he had come to power. Unable to tackle him directly, Ahmed Ben Bella tried to weaken him by cutting off his most loyal lieutenants. He attacked Ahmed Medeghri and removed the prefects from his authority. He provoked his resignation from the post of Minister of the Interior

---

18. Habib Souaïdia, *Procès de la sale guerre*, La Découverte, 2002, p. 114.

to take it up himself, and then forced the resignation of Gaïd Ahmed, Minister of Information. By December 1964, Ahmed Ben Bella was President of the Republic, Secretary General of the FLN, Head of Government, Minister of the Interior, Information and Finance.

The recommendations of the Soummam platform and collegial leadership, the fight against the cult of personality and respect for diversity were already a long way off. When, on May 28, 1965[19], he announced Abdelaziz Bouteflika's resignation as Foreign Minister at the Congress of Arab Heads of Government in Cairo, he had no idea that he was precipitating his own downfall.

Boumediene decided to take action after gathering his own clan. The coup took place on June 19, 1965. Boumediene arrested Ben Bella, after having his tanks take over the streets of the capital, to deal with any possible discontent among the population, since the deposed president, a great populist, had cultivated an image of a jovial president close to the people. At midday on the same day, Boumediene gave a speech on Algerian radio, announcing the creation of a Revolutionary Council.

Ahmed Ben Bella remained in prison for fifteen years, and was released only after the death of Colonel Boumediene, by his successor Chadli Bendjeddid, on October 30 1980.

---

19. Benjamin Stora, *Histoire de l'Algérie depuis l'indépendance*, La Découverte, 1994, p. 31.

II

BOUMEDIENE'S ALGERIA (1965-1978)

1. AFTER THE COUP

Colonel Boumediene's coup de force against Ahmed Ben Bella came as no surprise to many in the overt and covert opposition. During Ben Bella's three-year reign, his fellow travelers constantly warned him of his own excesses and Boumediene's intentions to seize power.

For Boumediene, it was necessary to quickly demonstrate his intransigence towards any form of opposition. Demonstrations organized by Ben Bella loyalists in several Algerian towns were put down in bloodshed, followed by waves of arrests. Some loyalists were tortured to death, while others were sent to dungeons for years.

Torture, as a deterrent policy, became a system: fear took hold and the letters "SM" became taboo. Boumediene ruled with an iron fist for thirteen years, and the slightest hint of opposition or questioning of his policies was considered a deviation from the principles of Novembre (referring to November [1] 1954, the date of the outbreak of the war of independence). Boumediene relied on the CNRA to consolidate his power. Thanks to the duplicity of his regime, Algeria appeared to be one of the leaders of the Third World, supporting major international causes and helping the liberation movements of African countries; at the same time, the regime in power favored the development of clientele and corruption. Everything was done to give the outside world the image of a freedom-loving country; corruption was even tolerated, but the nature of the regime was not to be touched.

2. THE ABORTIVE 1967 PUTSCH AND THE ASSASSINATION OF KRIM BELKACEM

Boumediene's dictatorship set out to restrict all freedoms: freedom of association and freedom of the press were banned, driving the opposition underground. Boumediene's authoritarian drift drove even his closest companions to revolt. In December 1967, army chief of staff Colonel Tahar Zbiri, one of the participants in the coup d'état of June 19, 1965, tried in turn to overthrow

Boumediene, but failed. Colonel Tahar Zbiri[20] brought to light a dispute that has always plagued the ranks of the Algerian army, namely the predominance of former French army personnel[21]. The latter deserted in the twilight of the Algerian War and joined the ranks of the ALN. Colonel Tahar Zbiri and other officers who had taken up arms in the early days of the Algerian War of Independence believed that these ex-French army deserters were there to infiltrate the Algerian army and, when the time came, turn it away from the homeland in favor of French interests. But Boumediene considered the matter closed, and would not go back on what had been decided in 1964, namely the incorporation of these former deserters into the new Algerian army. This is what prompted Colonel Tahar Zbiri to take up arms against his leader. Boumediene used the air force to bomb Tahar Zbiri's troops at the gates of El-Affroun, some sixty kilometers from Algiers. Zbiri went into exile and did not return until after Boumediene's death. It was his successor, Chadli Bendjeddid, who pardoned him from his 1969 death sentence. Colonel Saïd Abid, head of the 1st military region, who had refused to carry out Boumediene's order to engage his units against those of Tahar Zbiri, was found dead in his office.

The failed putsch and Khider's assassination marked the temporary death knell for the opposition, but it was to re-emerge in other forms. The following year, student

----

20. Lahouari Addi, *L'Algérie et la démocratie*, La Découverte, 1994, p. 59.
21. These are the Deserters of the French Army (DAF).

protests broke out under the aegis of the Union Nationale des Étudiants Algériens (UNEA), and repression soon followed: many activists were arrested, tortured and deported. The UNEA was dissolved in 1971.

Soaking up all this political effervescence, Krim Belkacem created the Mouvement Démocratique Républicain Algérien (MDRA) to return to the Algerian political scene. But this move could not escape the vigilance of Boumediene, who was wary of his former leader. Krim Belkacem represented a real danger to Boumediene: a former military leader, he was also the main negotiator of the Evian agreements. He was regarded by many foreign chancelleries as a credible figure, and some saw him as a democratic alternative to Boumediene.

On October 20, 1970, Krim Belkacem was found strangled with his own tie in a Düsseldorf hotel. The German police accused the Algerian secret service of being behind the murder. The three assassins had left incriminating documents in a briefcase abandoned at the airport luggage office. Among them was H'Mida Ait Mesbah, head of the operational military security service, who had fomented a false coup attempt and set a trap for Krim Belkacem.

3. Boumediene's reforms

The coup d'état of June 1965 saw the advent of a military bureaucracy made up of players with no past, and above all the sidelining of those who had been directly responsible for starting the war against France.

The successive eliminations of former personalities of the War of Independence (Mohamed Khider, Krim Belkacem) by Boumediene's henchmen belonging to the notorious Military Security, and the repression of all other political currents (communists, Berberists, former nationalists) enabled him to establish his regime.

In economic terms, the Boumediene regime opted for a centralized, dirigiste economy. The State was the main economic player, responsible for financing and redistributing income. Although it took some twenty years and the second oil crisis of 1986 to realize the reigning mismanagement, certain achievements nevertheless remained positive, boosted by export and budget revenues. Free schooling and medical care, for example, gave access to entire sections of society. The nationalization of hydrocarbons on February 24, 1971 enabled Algeria to benefit, from 1973 onwards[22], from a real income, which was however poorly used and above all unequally redistributed.

Industrial policy was a failure: it led to over-protection of state-owned companies through price controls, a low interest rate policy resulting in negative real interest rates, and measures to restrict imports. The result was extensive growth, to the detriment of productivity. Above all, the myth of industrialization allowed corruption to flourish on a

---

22. Date of the first oil shock.

massive scale. Contracts for the creation of turnkey companies enabled crooked bureaucrats to enrich themselves. These companies, lacking technology transfer, rigorous management and economic vision, were never profitable. Above all, they became indebted to the Treasury, increasing the budget deficit and feeding the money printing press. They were closed down years later, putting hundreds of thousands of people out of work.

The famous agrarian revolution decided upon in the early 1970s, against all economic logic, under the pompous slogan of "The land belongs to whoever works it", with the nationalization of agricultural land and the creation of cooperatives, introduced the civil service. This agricultural policy was an economic and human disaster. Algeria has become one of the world's biggest importers of durum wheat, even though it was considered by the Romans to be the empire's "granary[23]", and delivered large quantities of cereals to France before colonization. Food self-sufficiency remains a mirage: until the early 2000s, Algeria imported around $3 billion worth of agricultural products. Some economists believe that this astronomical sum is due not only to the high price of these products, but also to their detour to private interests.

In human terms, hundreds of thousands of peasants have left the countryside for the city, in search of an improbable El Dorado. They swelled the ranks of the destitute on the

---

23. *Annuaire de l'Afrique du Nord (1984)*, p. 534.

outskirts of the big cities. Unemployment, the housing crisis and demographic pressure led to the creation of hundreds of shanty towns.

4. The National Charter and the first armed Islamist insurrection

On June 19, 1975, in a televised speech celebrating his ten years in power, Boumediene announced the launch of a preliminary draft of the National Charter. In April 1976, at a cost of millions of dinars in advertising, he launched the campaign: he organized popular meetings in every town and village to reflect on and enrich the preliminary draft.

On June 27, 1976, the National Charter was adopted with over 98% of the vote. It enshrined socialism as the one and only alternative for the country's development: "Socialism means nothing other than a radical transformation of Algerian society, which implies the elimination of interests in opposition to the higher interests of the Algerian people", explained the President.

On November 17, 1976, the Algerian people voted for a new Constitution, of which the National Charter was the key element. On December 10, 1976, Colonel Boumediene was elected President of the Republic, regaining the legitimacy he had lacked. This election coincided with the emergence of an Islamist protest movement led by Abdellatif Soltani, who had already made his position on Boumediene's policies known in a 1974 manifesto[24]. Abdellatif Soltani belonged to the Ulemas movement and saw himself as a continuation of the thinking of Sheikhs Bachir El Ibrahimi and Mosbah, his predecessors at the head of this movement, who died under house arrest. He declared his categorical rejection of the new Constitution, which he described as a communist conspiracy against the identity of the Algerian people. This statement echoed that made twelve years earlier by the QIYAM association[25], which had condemned Nasser's execution of Sayeb Qotb in 1966.

This Islamist opposition led to the existence for the first time in the Mitidja mountains of an Islamist group carrying out acts of sabotage against public property, under the leadership of a certain Mahfoudh Nahnah. Nahnah was arrested by the security services, brought before the Blida court and imprisoned. He was released by Boumediene's successor, Colonel Chadli Bendjeddid, and became the leader of an Islamist party participating in the ruling coalition. He died on June 20, 2003.

5. BOUMEDIENE'S DEATH

Between 1976 and 1978, Boumediene devoted himself to his own revolution. Every project bore his signature. State

---

24. Benjamin Stora, *op. cit.* p. 56.
25. Arabist wing of the ulama.

television never missed a single one of his appearances. The cult of personality was at its height during this period. However, these two years also marked the start of the conflict between Algeria and Morocco over the Sahrawi question. A conflict which, through the stupidity of men, was to prevent, thirty years later, the creation of a Maghreb citizenship space.

In early November 1978, rumors began to circulate that the President's health was deteriorating, and that he had become seriously ill on his return from a visit to Syria on September 23, 1978. What's more, the President's image had completely disappeared from the television screen. The Algerian people fell back on Radio Tangier, the most widely listened-to radio station, which had of course been serving Moroccan propaganda since the start of the Saharan conflict.

On December 27, 1978, radio and television broadcasts were interrupted to make way for the reading of the Koran, and then to officially announce the death of President Boumediene. Rabah Bitat, president of the Assemblée Populaire Nationale, became acting president for forty-five days, before handing over to Chadli Bendjeddid. The funeral address at Boumediene's burial was delivered by Abdelaziz Bouteflika, his fellow traveler and confidant.

III

FROM THE ADVENT OF CHADLI BENDJEDDID TO THE RIOTS OF OCTOBER 1988 (1979-1988)

1. THE WAR OF SUCCESSION

The old demons resurfaced again, but this time in a war within the same clan, that of Oujda. The question of succession led to a splintering of the group. Bouteflika's speech on the day of Boumediene's funeral was already seen as a sign of this malaise.

Two succession scenarios were possible. The first was for the FLN apparatus to take power, in this case through Mohamed Salah Yahiaoui, its Secretary General; but the military chiefs did not want him, because they found him very conservative. The other candidate was Abdelaziz Bouteflika, Minister of Foreign Affairs and Boumediene's successor and confidant, who was considered to be very liberal. But the military chiefs, led by Colonel Kasdi Merbah, head of Military Security, and Colonel Hadjeres, head of the 5th Military Region, imposed a third thief: Colonel Chadli Bendjeddid, as the oldest officer in the highest rank. The induction ceremony took place at ENITA, the army's engineering school, then headed by Larbi Belkheir. Chadli Bendjeddid was appointed Secretary General of the FLN, and in February 1979 became President of the Republic.

Above all, this consensus enabled the military[26] to eliminate two of the regime's strongmen, Abdelaziz Bouteflika and Mohamed Salah Yahiaoui. This election marked the crumbling and subsequent break-up of the Oujda clan, with disastrous consequences for the country's future.

Several interest groups gravitating around the decision-making centers were formed, sponsored above all by high-ranking army officers, and they monopolized - and still monopolize - institutional life. Membership criteria are based neither on positive lobbying nor on any socio-economic vision, but on tribal, regionalist, clientelist and purely mercantile criteria. Disagreements between certain groups, or between powerful elements within these groups, over the distribution of rents and commissions for contracts with foreign companies, result in frequent

---

26. Khaled Nezzar, *Échec à une régression programmée*, Publisud, 2001, p. 234.

ministerial reshuffles, and appointments of ambassadors, prefects and managing directors of public companies. These raptors plunged the country into endless mourning, preceded by several events that heralded the catastrophe of the last decade.

2. Bendjeddid's restructuring of the secret services

Chadli Bendjeddid's accession to power meant, as for his predecessors and successors, the arrival of new men (future generals Belkheir and Mediene, known as "Toufik[27]", trained at the KGB school, among others), and consequently the departure of others. This led to resistance and struggles at the top, holding the Algerian people hostage.

All the events that followed, spontaneous or not, just or not, were subject to manipulation. The strongmen in power have used them to dismiss those who have fallen from grace, and at the same time to try to discredit any protest movement, the main concern being that none of their many privileges should one day be called into question.

President Chadli Bendjeddid attacked Boumediene's men in the secret services. The first "Malgache[28]" to pay the price was Kasdi Merbah, head of Military Security since independence. He was sidelined, appointed Secretary

---

27. *Le Monde interactif,* "Des généraux au cœur du pouvoir", July 2001.
28. The name given to former members of the MALG.

General of the Ministry of Defense, and replaced by his deputy, Lieutenant-Colonel Noureddine Zerhouni, founder of the Action Service. Zerhouni, in turn, was dismissed and sent far from Algiers, first as ambassador to Mexico and then to Washington in 1987. The Directorate of Military Security was entrusted to Lakhal Ayat from 1982 to 1987, when it split in two, with the Directorate General of Prevention and Security (DGPS), headed by Lakhal Ayat, and the Directorate of Army Security Control (DCSA), entrusted to Mohamed Betchine. The separation of the two departments will give Lakhal Ayat the investigative powers that had been the exclusive preserve of the DCSA.

The aim of this restructuring was to limit the exorbitant power of the Sécurité Militaire and, above all, that of those most loyal to the former head of the SM, Kasdi Merbah, within the DCSA. This transfer of power from one service to another created a conflict over the role of each structure, which grew over the years. This in turn led to a lack of awareness and control of the elements infiltrating each movement, including the Islamists. In fact, during the trial between General Nezzar and Second Lieutenant Habib Souaïdia in Paris in July 2002, a former secret service officer, Colonel Samraoui[29], described the difficulties encountered in dealing with infiltrators[30].

------

29. Habib Souaïdia, *op. cit.* p. 234.
30. Mohamed Samraoui, *Chroniques des années de sang*, Denoël, 2003, p. 87.

3. The FLN's headlong rush

The FLN, created at the dawn of the War of National Liberation to bring together the various Algerian political tendencies and put an end to the discord that reigned within the Movement for the Triumph of Democratic Liberties (MTLD) between the supporters of the old nationalist leader Messali El Hadj and the centralists (to whom were added the members of the secret organization, the armed wing of the MTLD and militants from other political formations such as the UDMA, the Ulemas and the Communist Party), became the FLN party.

Successive political failures (the eight-day strike in Algiers in January 1956, the assassination of Abane Ramdane, the failure of the GPRA in its fratricidal struggle against the army general staff, the arrival in power of Ben Bella and then Boumediene) meant that major political decisions were always taken outside the party. The military in power used the party as a civilian front: it served above all to attract all kinds of clientele in search of a seat on the bench. A unifying movement at its birth, it soon became the model par excellence of the single party. The party's governing bodies extol the socialist model, but the policy applied is one of bureaucratic capitalism, leading to the privatization of the State. It's an exclusive party, subservient to the military and able to channel the masses. As a vehicle for the "pensée unique", and a retrograde party in its orientation, it will drift from strength to strength, cutting itself off from the majority of Algerians: as the younger members do not recognize themselves in the party, it will become fossilized. The youngest Algerians did not recognize themselves in it, and it became fossilized. Those who joined it came to claim a social benefit, a pension, an import or vehicle license, a trade register... In 1979, the FLN's fourth congress enshrined the ideology of pan-Arabism for Algeria.

To carry out this work, Mohamed Messaadia was co-opted as the party's top official. He was chosen for his Nasserite ideas[31]. The party became the sole voice of the Algerian people.

The famous article 120 of the party's statutes, promulgated at the fourth session of the FLN Central Committee on December 24, 1980, was designed to control associative life and tame other political currents. It stipulated that a person had to be a member of the FLN party to be elected or to represent a mass organization. This caused a veritable panic among the left-wing movement, and first and foremost among Communist Party activists who, after the adoption of the National Charter in 1976, had made mass organizations the preferred place for propagating Marxist ideas. These left-wing militants found themselves obliged to redeploy, and chose student collectives to make their ideas prevail.

---

31. In reference to the former Egyptian head of state, Djamel Abdel Nasser.

4. Berber Spring

The so-called "Berber Spring" of 1980 was merely the natural progression of a citizen's demand that had been born in the Algerian nationalist movement before the war, but which had not yet reached fruition. The Algerian nationalist movement (Étoile Nord-Africaine, ENA) emerged among French immigrants in 1924, and included Kabyle workers among its founders. These same Kabyle workers went on to form the majority of the militants of the Algerian People's Party (PPA), the successor to the Étoile Nord-Africaine. Already in 1945, the nationalist movement had split between Messali Hadj, leader of the nationalist movement and supporter of an "Arab-Muslim Algeria", and those who militated for an "Algerian Algeria" respecting its diversity, including its Berber identity. The latter were expelled on charges of "Berber-materialism".

The outbreak of the war of national liberation put the question of identity on the back burner. After independence, the powers that be denied Algeria's Berber identity. The 1963 Algiers Charter, the National Charter and the 1976 Constitution made no reference to it. But history is bigger than men. The "Berber Spring", founded on a just cause, shook the regime to its foundations and paved the way for protests. The ban on Dr Mouloud Mammeri, writer and anthropologist, from giving a lecture on ancient Kabyle poetry in Tizi Ouzou, for example, got out of hand: Dr Mouloud Mammeri, invited by the students' committee of the Tizi Ouzou university campus, was intercepted at a police checkpoint and taken to the office of the wilaya secretary-general. He was told that he could not give his lecture, giving as a spurious reason the "risk of disturbing public order".

On hearing the news, the students gathered in a general assembly and decided to demonstrate to express their anger. The demonstrations continued over the following days. The population, at first curious and above all fearful, joined in with the students: the flow of demonstrators grew, and the slogans gradually became more radical; the demand for Amazighité (Berberity), initially carried by militant students, touched all sectors of society. From being a linguistic issue, it became a civic one. Workers went on strike, shopkeepers lowered their curtains, students and teachers occupied campuses. High school students boycotted classes. The medical and paramedical professions took their turn to occupy the hospital. Demonstrations followed one another. On April 7, the movement's leaders took their demands to Algiers. The demonstrators headed for the presidency. Security forces descended on them. Dozens were arrested and others injured.

On April 16, the city was paralyzed by a general strike. The cultural demand became a denunciation of the dictatorship and a quest for democracy. But the illegitimate dictatorship in power, with no understanding of the virtues of dialogue, used force. On the night of April 19-20, riot police and gendarmerie forces, backed by the army, took over the university campus and housing estate, the headquarters of striking companies and the hospital. The police crackdown left dozens injured. Twenty-four leaders of the Berber cultural movement were arrested, brought before the state security court in Médéa and charged with undermining state security.

The powers that be, true to form, never learned a lesson. Chadli Bendjeddid used a legitimate demand for recognition of the Amazigh identity of the Algerian people to get rid of Kasdi Merbah, head of Military Security, who was accused of passivity towards his native region. He was replaced by Lakhal Ayat.

The police also approached some of the leaders of the 1980 "Berber Spring" to divide the movement. The damage was considerable and is still visible some twenty years later.

5. The rise of Islamism

The rise of Islamism in Algeria during the 1980s is a clear reality affecting all sectors of society. It was the result of a combination of international and national events.

The advent of the Islamic Republic in Iran in 1979 prompted the West to revise its geostrategic system, in the face of what was termed the "green peril". This event influenced almost all Islamist movements in the world at the time, particularly in the Arab world. This new form of expression of Islam, a revolutionary Islam embodied by Ayatollah Khomeini, prompted Western countries (through their intelligence services) to lean on their Saudi allies and organize Wahhabi propaganda (in Wahhabism, Shiites are considered impious, even impostors), but also to lean on secular Iraq to confront Iran militarily. A merciless war ensued, lasting eight years and claiming a million lives.

The Saudis also acted as an appendage to the West during the Russian invasion of Afghanistan in the early 1980s. They organized jihad propaganda throughout the Muslim world, relying on a system of charities affiliated mainly to Wahhabism. In the 1990s, one of the GIA emirs from the Mitidja region was trained in armed combat for two years in Saudi Arabia before going to Afghanistan.

Like all Muslim countries, Algeria experienced the same turbulence, propaganda and manipulation by the secret services involved in these maneuvers on the eve of the new world order.

In his book, Colonel Samraoui accuses the DRS of having put one of its lieutenants in charge of *El Hijra oua Takfir* ("Exile and Atonement") in the 1980s. The powers that be, devoid of any geopolitical vision, allowed everything to go astray. This gave rise to a profusion of charitable associations, the origin of funds for which remains uncertain. With the goodwill of the powers that be, networks have been set up to send young Algerians to faraway Afghanistan to wage jihad. These "freedom fighters" would return a decade later to wage jihad in their own country. Of course, any self-respecting police state will infiltrate these "Afghans", hoping to manipulate them when the time is right.

The Algerian regime, bogged down in its contradictions, permissive at times, manipulative at others, always policing and repressive, thinking it had settled temporal issues by muzzling the opposition and different currents of thought with statutory articles, set about appropriating Islam by nationalizing it. Imams were paid by the State to preach the virtues of socialism. Some civil servant imams have not hesitated to assert in their sermons that Islam conveys socialist ideas, or that Islam and socialism represent two sides of the same coin. They illustrated this with the example of the apostle Abudher El Ghofari, nicknamed "Abudher the Socialist".

But other independent imams, often young, from working-class backgrounds, close to Islamist circles, have developed a completely different discourse, castigating government policy. This radical discourse was to be emulated by more and more people. The failure of the FLN state, symbolized by the multi-dimensional crisis faced by the Algerian people, allowed the Islamist movement to expand.

In university circles, the Islamist movement was gaining momentum; those disappointed with Arabization formed the bulk of the troops, hijacking and spoiling the Algerian education system. Arabist students ended up with diplomas that led straight to unemployment, while the sons of regime dignitaries who advocated Arabization of the education system sent their children to study at

European or American universities. Thus, two clandestine ideological movements with diametrically opposed ideas clashed on campuses and university halls of residence: on the one hand, left-wing organizations, led by men from the Communist Party, and on the other, Islamist militants. The conflicts were manifold and encompassed a wide range of subjects, such as the organization of university housing committees, the place of the Arabic language in teaching, places of worship, morals, the banning of cultural events, pedagogical issues...

Attacks multiplied, encouraged by the manipulations of the security services who had infiltrated the student collectives. This later legitimized the presence of these same police forces on university campuses, under the pretext of maintaining order and safeguarding public buildings, followed by the prohibition of any activity not falling within the so-called "legal" framework.

In the autumn of 1982, the campus confrontation took a further step forward. A student, Amzal Kamel, was murdered at Ben Aknoun University, triggering a campaign of arrests in Islamist circles and culminating in the famous rally at the central faculty initiated by Abassi Madani (later to become president of the FIS, the Islamic Salvation Front), Sheikhs Abdellatif Soltani and Sahnoun to denounce the harassment of Islamist militants in the university environment. But the December 11, 1982 rally soon turned into a confrontation with the security services, leading to the arrest of the protest's initiators. Abassi Madani was arrested and imprisoned, and Sheikhs Soltani and Sahnoun were placed under house arrest. Ahmed Merah[32], Bouyali's right-hand man, said that Bouyali had warned Abassi Madani against such a gathering, knowing that it would enable the security services to identify anonymous people. Ahmed Merah became one of General Smaïn Lamari's men in the 1990s, which enabled him to enter the business world. But after a stint in Serkadji prison in 2003, a sentence that should have served as a warning, he was murdered.

Bouyali, an early Islamist militant and former officer in the National Liberation Army, took up arms in April 1982 and began organizing what would later become the famous Bouyali maquis. He had already carried out an attack on gendarmes in Ben Aknoun on November 17, 1982. On January 3, 1983, his brother was killed by the security services in reprisal. The Bouyali affair had just begun and lasted four years. He was shot dead on January 3, 1987 by security forces on the Larbaa road in Blida. He had been denounced by his own driver and friend, who had been turned over by the security services. This case was first tried in April 1985 by the Medéa security court, following the first dismantling of the group. The second trial took place in 1987, when two hundred people, including the seventeen most active elements, were put on trial. They had all been arrested during the operation of October 22, 1985. Among them were Mansouri Meliani (future first

---

32. Based on his book *L'Affaire Bouyali*, Algiers, à compte d'auteur, 1998, p. 45.

From the Advent of Chadli Bendjeddid to the Riots of October 1988 (1979-1988)

emir of the Armed Islamic Group), Abdelkader Chebouti (future first emir of the Islamic State Movement), Azedinne Baa and Abderahmane Hattab. Heavy sentences were handed down, in particular against Bouyali, sentenced to life imprisonment in absentia.

On April 16, 1984, over ten thousand people attended the funeral of Sheikh Soltani, who had died under house arrest. A few days later, in the face of this demonstration of strength by the Islamist movement, the Popular National Assembly adopted the famous Family Code. Pure coincidence?

To calm things down further, and avoid swelling the ranks of the Bouyali maquis, Chadli Bendjeddid decided to release Abassi Madani, after some of his former comrades in arms from the war of independence had pleaded his case with him.

6. The social revolts of 1985 in Algiers, and 1986 in Constantine and Sétif

Populist socialism produced a privileged caste who ostentatiously flaunted their ill-gotten wealth, while the Algerian people sank deeper and deeper into misery. The FLN was discredited by business and bureaucracy. The Soviet-inspired economic development model chosen in the wake of independence, with its emphasis on heavy industry, required huge amounts of capital, which oil provided.

In the early 1980s, Algeria was indebted due to low domestic savings, and was still dependent on oil revenues, which accounted for over 95% of its exports. State-owned companies were economically failing and the private sector non-existent. In 1984[33], Algeria imported 64% of dairy products, 60% of cereals and 80% of pulses. The two oil counter-shocks of 1983 and 1986 led to a drop in foreign currency earnings and plunged Algeria into crisis, marking the end of the welfare state that guaranteed purchasing power and provided jobs. As needs increased tenfold, accentuated by demographic pressure, it became impossible to repay the debt and import products (food, pharmaceuticals, spare parts, etc.), provoking growing social unrest.

From the early 1980s onwards, two hundred thousand people entered the job market every year, to which must be added the million unemployed inherited from the 1970s. The quality of education was deteriorating, and illiteracy was on the rise: after nine years of basic education, some pupils could neither read nor write. The free medical system was crumbling: doctors were underpaid; medicines were running out; water-borne diseases, which had regressed for a while, were reappearing; strike followed strike. Not to mention the fact that the elite were gradually fleeing the country: almost half the doctors in the 1988 graduating class of the Algiers medical school went into exile, most of them to France.

---

33. *Annuaire de l'Afrique du Nord (1985)*, p. 584.

Lack of housing led to promiscuity: parents slept next to their children, balconies and cellars were turned into makeshift accommodation, and in some families, people even took turns sleeping. The age of marriage receded. Young people had no space for freedom, and leisure activities were non-existent. In and around Algiers, one of the main occupations of young and old alike was to watch for the arrival of water, day and night. Water was available once or twice a week, if not less, and often at dawn. Sometimes, to make matters worse, only the lower floors of the buildings were supplied, due to lack of pressure. The other occupation was to queue for hours on end outside the entrances to the state-owned shopping malls, hoping for a hypothetical price-controlled food product. Given the slim chance of being served, it was better to be young and in good health.

The rest of the time, most young people were busy doing nothing. These idlers from working-class neighborhoods were nicknamed "hittists", literally "those who spend their time leaning against a wall". Their main occupation was smoking joints and dreaming of faraway lands. The rest fell into the informal economy, also known as "trabendo". The failing state economy led to a flight of capital into these parallel circuits, which regime pundits took advantage of to recycle corruption money. The trabendistes flourished, as did the "sheep". Their approach was simple: obtain an entry visa for a country on the northern shore of the Mediterranean (France, Spain, Italy), or, for the more daring, for a distant country (Turkey, Taiwan), or sometimes for neighboring Morocco. Then you had to choose a type of merchandise that was easy to sell (perfume, lingerie, telephony and accessories, spare parts), and make contacts with a corrupt customs officer - and there was no shortage of that. Indeed, some customs officers had the luxury of driving around in cars costing 30,000 euros, even though their monthly payments did not exceed 150 euros. After a prior agreement on the commission of these crooked officials, the imported goods crossed the border without being checked and, of course, no tax was paid.

The big traffickers, on the other hand, didn't travel: they organized their traffic by recruiting "sheep", young beginners to whom they paid the trip, the stay if necessary, and a small salary.

Then at the highest level, the caïds, who lived like sultans worthy of the era of the Umayyad caliphs, regularly imported dozens of cars and containers filled with goods of all kinds. But they had to act with the blessing of one of the regime's top brass or one of its offspring. The most famous example in Algiers was that of Mouhouche, a young man from the working-class district of Bourouba, friend and accomplice of Toufik, son of the then President of the Republic, Chadli Bendjeddid. Thanks to this cover, he benefited from bank loans that not even public companies could hope for. The famous Mouhouche was nicknamed "Testosa" by the children of his neighborhood: this unfortunate man couldn't even pronounce the name of his Ferrari Testa

Rosa, parked at the foot of dilapidated buildings inhabited by people who couldn't afford the daily bread and milk.

When this affair was brought to light to put pressure on President Chadli Bendjeddid in the late 1980s, Mouhouche was arrested and sentenced to twelve years' imprisonment. As for the president's son, he took refuge with his uncle, ambassador to Venezuela, in order to be forgotten. (This affair was exploited during the coup d'état of January 1992, as one of the means of pressure exerted on Chadli Bendjeddid to force him to resign).

Meanwhile, company strikes multiplied: social revolts began. The first, in the Casbah district of Algiers, lasted four days, from April 23 to 27, 1985. Violent clashes broke out between local residents and the police, following the collapse of a dilapidated building. This revolt was followed, a year later, by those in Sétif and Constantine (November 8-12, 1986), where the population joined the high school and university students who took to the streets to express their anger at the high cost of living. These two events seemed to herald the tremors of October 1988. But instead of providing just answers to a population in distress, the leaders were busy consolidating their networks and protecting their privileges. Thus, just after the first oil counter-shock in 1983, Chadli Bendjeddid decided to elevate certain senior army officers to the rank of general, a rank that had never before existed in the Algerian army. Among these appointments were Khaled Nezzar, future Minister of Defense and mastermind of the

January 1992 putsch, Abdellah Belhouchet, future Army Chief of Staff and prime mover behind the October 1988 crackdown, Belloucif and Belkheir.

7. THE MURDER OF LAWYER ALI MECILI

When power panics, it kills; its preferred target is grey matter armed with its pen. On April 7, 1987, the corrupt rulers targeted lawyer Ali Mecili, a close associate of FFS leader Hocine Ait Ahmed. He was, among others, behind the meeting organized between two former leaders of the war of independence, Hocine Ait Ahmed and Ahmed Ben Bella. These two political leaders were invited to bury their battle axes and reflect on a democratic alternative to the current government.

The secret services have decided to add Ali Mecili to the long list of murdered political opponents. The chosen murderer was a notorious gangster, pimp and hitman by the name of Abdelmalek Amalou. He was arrested in Paris two months later, and extradited to Algiers after being held in police custody for 48 hours by Charles Pasqua. He was carrying an Algerian secret service pass authorizing him to travel in military zones. The pass was signed by Captain Hassani, the right-hand man of Lakhal Ayat, head of Military Security during those years. In his testimony[34],

---

34. Interview with *Nouvel Observateur*, June 14, 2001.

Hichem Aboud reported that, in exchange, Amalou received 800,000 francs and an apartment in Algiers.

Lakhal Ayat found himself mentioned by chance in the case of Colonel Chabou[35]. Chabou died in a helicopter accident (a Puma recently acquired from France) on his way to a meeting with a Russian officer in Lakhal Ayat's office, where Khaled Nezzar and Selim Saadi were also supposed to be. The latter was supposed to be on board the helicopter, but preferred to make the journey by car. In his memoirs, Nezzar recalls that he himself had taken charge of Chabou's guest, the Russian general Kuruchin, on the evening of his death.

Selim Saadi became head of the 3rd military region at the height of the crisis with Morocco, with Khaled Nezzar as his deputy. Together, they opposed the appointment of Chadli Bendjeddid as President of the Republic in 1979, but were outvoted. When Boudiaf died in 1992, Selim Saadi became Minister of the Interior.

Master Ali Mecili's background may well explain why he was murdered. A former intelligence officer during and after the war of independence, he was known for his organizational skills. His assassination came at a time when a wind of democracy was beginning to blow across totalitarian regimes in general, and in Eastern Europe in particular. Was it this fear that prompted the powers that be to liquidate one of the masterminds of the Front des

---

35. Khaled Nezzar, *Échec à une régression programmée, op. cit.* p. 199.

Forces Socialistes, creator of "Libre Algérie", who, only a few days before his death, had just accused the Algerian regime of turning the country into a terrorist territory[36]? Or is there another reason? In 1989, Khaled Derbal, a Benbellist militant who had frequented the milieu of the 18th arrondissement a few years earlier, was assassinated because he was very interested in the agenda of Mecili's last days[37]. This may explain why Algeria reacted with an official communiqué to Amalou's extradition in 1987, speaking of an extradition of a hoodlum with no connection whatsoever with the lawyer's death. On November 27, 1987, two French hostages were released in Lebanon. Algeria was at the "heart of the negotiations", as Charles Pasqua put it.

8. THE RIOTS OF OCTOBER 1988

Algeria could not remain outside the wave of change that swept almost the entire planet at the end of the 1980s. Secret service reports helped Chadli Bendjeddid become aware of the new era of democracy emerging in Eastern Europe.

One of the first measures taken was to relax the law on associations: on July 21, 1987, the FLN's tutelage was lifted. But this was not enough.

---

36. Reporters sans frontières, *op. cit.* p. 95.
37. *Ibid*, p. 93.

In the run-up to the FLN congress, Chadli Bendjeddid commissioned Mouloud Hamrouche to reflect on the subject. Among the ideas put forward was the legalization of certain political parties that already had a popular base.

Faced with this programmed end of the single party and a possible reshaping of the political landscape, certain pillars of the regime and the horde of scavengers gravitating around them were going to be alarmed: they would make the elimination of their adversaries a priority in order to save their rents and privileges. Thus, the 1987-1988 social year was one of conflict and backstabbing between the clans. The first to bear the brunt of this battle for control was General Mustapha Belloucif, who a year earlier had been accused of embezzlement by his peers and sidelined. This sidelining was intended to weaken Chadli Bendjeddid, and dissuade him from standing for re-election to the party. Belloucif was accused of embezzling 38 million francs and 2.5 million dinars from state funds, but for him, the real reason was his refusal to sign a six-billion-franc contract with France for air cover equipment in 1984[38]. Added to this was his failure to authorize the use of French airspace during the Chad conflict, and his refusal to carry out the order to quell citizen protests in the east in 1985.

General Belhouchet, his deputy, took over his post, much to the delight of his close friend Messaadia, Chadli Bendjeddid's FLN successor. Messaadia and Belhouchet

---

38. Abdelhamid Brahimi, *Aux origines de la tragédie algérienne (1958-2000)*, Hoggar Press, 2001, p. 220-221.

had taken part together in the abortive assassination attempt on Ferhat Abbas, then president of the GPRA: they were pardoned and later recovered by Boumediene.

Faced with this defection of a very close friend, Chadli Bendjeddid saw fit to use another joker, calling on Nezzar, who owed him his career and whom he had appointed to head the ground forces. In 1958, Belloucif and Nezzar had taken their first steps in the Armée de Libération Nationale (ALN) alongside Chadli Bendjeddid, their superior[39]. The former had left school to join the maquis, while the latter was a deserter from the French army and needed protection, which he found in Chadli Bendjeddid, at a time when in other sections and companies, some were suffering humiliation at the hands of ordinary soldiers who saw them as moles. (This decision proved fatal for the President, since it was this foal who deposed him in January 1992).

This appointment strengthened Bendjeddid in his position, but did not prevent a clan war from breaking out, especially between Larbi Belkheir and Mouloud Hamrouche, two people close to Chadli Bendjeddid (one was chief of staff at the presidency and the other secretary general at the presidency).

This led directly to the riots of October 1988, when the Algerian people once again paid with their blood for a war of interests between clans.

---

39. Khaled Nezzar, Mémoires du général Nezzar, Chihab Éditions, Algiers, 1999, p. 45.

Of course, some analysts - and we'll give them the benefit of the doubt - have put forward the hypothesis that these riots were the result of spontaneous anger, without any manipulation, expressed by the Algerian people in the face of their deteriorating purchasing power. But this hypothesis is refuted by a majority of analysts who take into consideration certain events that took place just before this tragedy, including Chadli Bendjeddid's famous speech urging the people to express their anger in the event that they felt they had been the victim of an injustice: "I don't understand anyone who goes to the butcher to buy meat, finds the price exorbitant and doesn't protest." Add to this the rumor circulating throughout Algiers a few days beforehand about the October 5 date, and all the strikes that broke out at almost the same time.

Of course, many questions remain unanswered almost eighteen years on, and no one dares to offer plausible explanations for all these coincidences, at the risk of ending up in court. Were the arsonists who planned the riots of October 5, 1988 overwhelmed by events? The toll was heavy: five hundred dead, killed by the murderous bullets of security forces anxious to protect public buildings. At least, that was the official explanation given by the killers, who considered that the life of a young Algerian was worthless in front of a cement building. In the early days of the revolt, these young people demonstrated in a very peaceful manner, wanting only to be given attention and to have their distress heard. But others decided otherwise.

So the instigators of this tragedy, by using their weapons to kill, have only radicalized these young people, pushing them towards extreme solutions.

The first victim was recorded on October 4 in Bachdjarrah, a working-class district on the outskirts of Algiers. On October 5, the demonstrations turned into a riot. Public buildings were ransacked. FLN party structures and police stations, symbols of contempt, repression and preferential treatment, were burned. Clashes between the security forces and the population claimed dozens of victims, most of them young people mowed down in the prime of life. That same evening, a state of siege was declared. Chadli Bendjeddid put General Nezzar in charge. Algiers was cordoned off by tanks, and calm was restored at the cost of hundreds of deaths, thousands of injuries and just as many arrests. Hundreds more were tortured in police stations, gendarmerie barracks and Military Security detention centers. The events of October 5 1988 were not confined to Algiers, but spread to many other Algerian cities.

Algeria's population was young, with around 70% under the age of 25. Most of those who took to the streets knew nothing of the Algerian army other than the glorious memories of the War of Independence. They discovered a brutal army, firing without warning on its own children; they discovered systematic torture, and leaders with fascist methods. The myth had been shattered.

The president went on state television in tears, promising a democratic opening. In the wake of the tragedy, major

From the Advent of Chadli Bendjeddid to the Riots of October 1988 (1979-1988)

changes took place at the head of the state. The head of the secret services, General Lakhal Ayat, was dismissed and replaced by General Betchine, while Toufik replaced the latter at the head of the Central Directorate of Military Security. Kasdi Merbah was appointed Prime Minister to implement the reforms promised by Chadli Bendjeddid, including the democratization of Algeria with the drafting of a new constitution. General Nezzar was appointed Chief of Staff in July 1989, replacing General Belhouchet, who followed his friend Messaadia into retirement. But this appointment led to protests from a number of generals and, above all, the resignation of General Kamel Abderahim.

IV

THE FALSE DEMOCRATIZATION PROCESS AND THE SECOND ALGERIAN WAR (1989-2007)

I have chosen to cover this vast period in one chapter, with the sole aim of showing that the heavy toll paid by the people over the last decade is the direct consequence of the ruling regime's firm opposition to any real democratic opening that would have challenged its privileges.

1. FROM OPENING TO COUP D'ÉTAT

Bendjeddid re-elected in February 1989

The air was very heavy to breathe throughout Algeria, and especially in Algiers. The people of Algiers did not want to forget the riots and massacre of October 1988. This event will remain buried in the collective memory for a long time to come. This martyrdom will be regularly recalled in the cries of demonstrators at every scuffle with the security services. Young supporters of soccer clubs in the Bab-El-Oued district would turn it into a song: *"Bab-El-Oued echouhada[40]"*.

In the arena of power, it's a mess. An incredible number of important dates have been announced by the President of the Republic in record time. Three major events stand out: the congress of the Front de Libération Nationale, the presidential election and the referendum on the new constitution. These three events took place in the space of four months.

In his account of this period[41], General Nezzar says he had reservations about one of the articles in the preliminary draft constitution presented by Mouloud Hamrouche just after October 5, 1988, in the presence of General Betchine. Article 40 of the Constitution, which opens the way to a multi-party system, was not worded in the way he described. This reflection already tells us something about how decision-makers viewed the political arena. The question arises: was the Constitution drafted before or after October 1988? This answer leads to others. Who was behind the events of October 1988 and the massacre that followed? Why provoke them? One thing is certain: during

---

40. "The martyrs of Bab-El-Oued."
41. Khaled Nezzar, *échec à une régression programmée, op. cit.* p. 138.

that summer, the President of the Republic took a three-month vacation on the Oranese coast. Fifteen years on, no precise answers have been forthcoming, apart from a polite reading of the events by those involved in the tragedy.

The congress confirmed Bendjeddid as Secretary General of the FLN and sole candidate in the presidential election, sweeping aside with one hand all the rumors previously circulating about his likely withdrawal in favor of other candidates, such as Taleb Ibrahimi and Messaadia.

On February 23, 1989, the new Constitution was adopted with 73.43% of the vote. A few days earlier, during a meeting of the Berber cultural movement, Saïd Saadi, alongside Ferhat M'henna, had announced the creation of the Rassemblement pour la Culture et la Démocratie (RCD), and on February 18, the idea of creating the Front Islamique du Salut (FIS) had been floated at the Sunna mosque in Bab-El-Oued. So, the idea of creating two parties with diametrically opposed ideologies was well and truly floated before the adoption of the new Constitution.

The creation of FIS

In his memoirs[42], Nezzar recounts a conversation with General Betchine about the creation of the FIS (Front Islamique du Salut): "General Betchine told me: 'Si, Khaled, c'est pour mieux les surveiller. This sentence sums it all up. This is the meaning of the project to create

---

42. Khaled Nezzar, *Mémoires du général Nezzar, op. cit.* p. 176.

the Front Islamique du Salut (Islamic Salvation Front). Colonel Samraoui[43], number two in Algerian counter-espionage until 1996, told the Paris court during the trial between sub-lieutenant Souaïdia and General Nezzar, under the watchful eye of the latter, that "the Algerian secret services had seventeen agents on the advisory board of the Islamic Salvation Front, out of the thirty-five members who made it up".

It's easy to see why the first FIS meeting took place on February 18, a week before the adoption of the new constitution allowing a multi-party system. After bedtime prayers on February 18, the Sunna mosque in Bab-El-Oued was packed with worshippers from all over the country. Word of mouth had heralded an important meeting. Almost the entire Islamist nomenklatura was present: Abassi Madani, Ali Benhadj, Zebda Benazouz, Hachemi Sahnouni, Abdelbaki Sahraoui (the imam assassinated in Paris), A. Djaballah (current leader of the Mouvement National du Renouveau), Ali Djeddi, Mohamed Saïd (assassinated by Zitouni in the maquis).

The question was: how to build a party that could represent the Islamist movement, with the aim of applying Islamic law in Algeria?

All the speakers tried to provide answers, using more religious preaching than political argumentation. When Abassi Madani took the floor, he developed an entirely different

---

43. Habib Souaïdia, *op. cit.* p. 272.

discourse: in addition to religious arguments (Koranic verses and words of the prophet), he returned to the declaration of November 1st 1954, which he would make one of his hobbyhorses throughout his tenure at the head of the FIS, to explain the need to create a party capable of defending the sacrifice of the martyrs of the war of national liberation. He felt that this sacrifice had been betrayed by successive governments since independence. He would often return to "the ideals of November 1954", and to the deviance suffered. But most of those present found his speech too philosophical, and didn't appreciate it.

When Mohamed Saïd (executed in the maquis by Djamel Zitouni, leader of the Armed Islamic Group on the eve of the presidential elections in November 1995) took the floor, a ruckus broke out inside the mosque, with some people trying to prevent him from speaking. But he was unimpressed and tried, in spite of everything, to give his point of view, which went against what the audience wanted to hear, since he considered the creation of a political party to be premature.

Hachemi Sahnouni took the floor just after Mohamed Saïd to castigate him, accusing him of colluding with the state, and of being against the emergence of the Party of God. These words prompted a few overheated people to advance towards Mohamed Saïd and hurl insults and threats at him. Ali Benhadj came to support Mohamed Saïd, interposing himself in front of Sahnouni's followers. Had it not been for his intervention, which succeeded in calming tempers, a lynching would undoubtedly have taken place. Immediately after this incident, Sahnouni took the floor again and issued a warning against all those who would dare hinder the formation of the FIS: "This party will see the light of day whatever Mohamed Saïd's opinion," he said. The "DRS preacher" was determined that orders should be carried out. Ali Djeddi and Abdellah Djaballah withdrew in protest at the way Mohamed Saïd had been treated.

On Friday March 10 1989, the FIS was born at the Ibn Badiss mosque in Kouba. Abdelbaki Sahraoui made the announcement to the faithful present during the day of prayer. But above all, we will remember the contradictions within the Islamist movement: some were absolutely not in favor of politicizing Islam. For example, the Salafists (followers of a rigorist Islam), who represented the majority current among the initiators of the Islamic Salvation Front, found themselves divided into two tendencies: the scientific Salafists considered participation in the political game to be contrary to Islamic law. These ideas were advocated by preachers Abdelmalek and Elaïd from the "La Colonne" mosque in Hydra. The fighting Salafists, better known as "jihadists", preached combat and jihad for the restoration of the caliphate.

This tendency was itself divided into two movements: the first considered that the democratic game, even if its aim was to establish an Islamic Republic, was completely contrary to the precepts of Islam that only jihad could fulfill, and that any participation in the political game was considered impious. This movement was called "*El Mouahidoun*", better known as "*El Hijra oua Takfir*", i.e. "Exile and Atonement". Its preacher was a former army officer, Dr. Ahmed Bouamra (killed by Algerian services in prison), a veteran of the Afghan war. The other "jihadist" movement was participationist. It considered that the use of a political party to establish an Islamic Republic was licit, but that once the Islamic Republic had been achieved, the party no longer had any reason to exist. This movement was represented by most of the preachers who worked to create the FIS, including Ali Benhadj and Sahnouni. It was this movement that managed to win over the majority of Salafists (even the "Afghans") and channel them.

As for the other current of thought, close to the Muslim Brotherhood with its three tendencies, namely Mahfoudh Nahnah's "internationalists", Mohamed Saïd's "Djazarists" and Djaballah's "Nahdaouis", it was against the idea of creating a party representing the Islamist movement on its own, all the more so as the initiators were Salafists. The latter considered that anyone advocating an ideology other than their own was unholy. Moreover, it countered the work of Sheikh Sahnoun's "Daawa" league, where this current of thought, close to the Muslim Brotherhood, was in the majority, while the Salafist current was virtually non-existent. The Salafists draw their jurisprudence from Saudi scholars, i.e. the Medinan school[44], while the Muslim

---

44. Medina is Islam's second holiest city.

Brothers draw their jurisprudence from Egyptian scholars, i.e. the El-Azhar school.

The Islamist movement has gone from two to six tendencies with the emergence of politics, and the gap between the different factions has widened daily.

On May 10 1989, Abassi Madani was appointed FIS president and sole spokesman by the Consultative Council. But during the summer of 1989, many conflicts broke out in the mosques over control of the various factions, under the passive and complicit eye of the security services.

The most deadly was at the El-Fath mosque in El-Harrach, on the outskirts of Algiers, where Salafists and Shiites clashed with sabres and axes. The police only intervened at the end of the confrontation to evacuate the injured. Several other similar incidents occurred throughout Algeria, in Constantine, Lakhdaria, Setif, Blida, and above all in Algiers, where Hachemi Sahnouni's militia reigned terror, even calling themselves the "Islamic police".

During the three years from 1989 to 1992, when the FIS was Algeria's leading political force, the militia linked to this preacher made headlines more than once: in high-profile cases such as the Linda De Susa affair, or the ban on Ait Menguelet singing at the Salle Atlas in Bab-El-Oued, or the punitive raids on university halls of residence... This militia would be at the top of its game with the creation of the GIA.

But since Bouyali's death and the disbanding of his group, the first to be tempted into armed action is Abdelkader Chakendi, better known as Abdelkader El Asnami. This preacher, a university graduate with a degree in literature and a former follower of the Muslim Brotherhood doctrine, made a name for himself in 1989 with the attack on the Blida court and prison, where he broke out some of his friends who had been arrested a few days earlier. In 1991, he became a paramilitary instructor for Sahnouni's militia, before the latter decided to set a trap for him, inviting him to Bouzereah to develop a guerrilla project. The security services were waiting for him, ready to catch him. Sensing the betrayal of a person who seemed suspicious, Chekendi had his route checked by third parties, who confirmed his doubts. He abandoned the Chréa mountains to settle in his hometown of Aïn Defla, where he was arrested a year later during the 1992 summer sweep. Sentenced to death, the first emir of an armed group has since been awaiting execution in Serkadji prison.

On August 22, 1989, the FIS, through Abassi Madani, submitted its legalization file to the Ministry of the Interior.

The repercussions of the turbulent summer of 1989 were not long in coming. Kasdi Merbah was relieved of his post as head of government, in favor of Mouloud Hamrouche, until then Secretary General of the Presidency. From an official point of view, Mouloud Hamrouche was in a better position to undertake the necessary reforms (a task he acquitted himself of suitably) and the talks with the International Monetary Fund and the World Bank to avoid Algeria having to reschedule its debt. But the real reason was Chadli Bendjeddid's conviction that Kasdi Merbah was a candidate to replace him as head of state. He was a man appreciated by foreign chancelleries, who overlooked his background as head of the secret services, as evidenced by the number of foreign delegations received and receptions organized in their honor.

Added to this were the changes made at the head of the army a few months earlier. When Chadli Bendjeddid installed Nezzar at the head of the army general staff in place of Belhouchet, he provoked the wrath of certain other generals, who let him know it: among them Yahia Rahal, Sadek Hadjress, Kamel Abderahim... The latter even asked for his retirement, seeing Chadli Bendjeddid's insistence on keeping Nezzar in his new post.

Zeroual's appointment[45] as head of the land forces was also controversial. Zeroual relinquished his position only a short time after his appointment, following a dispute with Nezzar over the army's restructuring program. During this episode, Chadli Bendjeddid once again pleaded Nezzar's cause.

General Zeroual was replaced by General Lamari. Paradoxically, a few years later, General Nezzar appointed General Zeroual in his place. Why him and not someone else? The answer is simple: before leaving the army in 1989, Zeroual apologized to General Nezzar. A few years later, certain events and factors, including Zeroual's desire for emancipation from Nezzar, would shed light on this vision of things. I'll come back to this later.

---

45. Khaled Nezzar, *Mémoires du général Nezzar, op. cit.* p. 169.

On September 14, 1989, Mouloud Hamrouche's government legalized the FIS. Algeria became the first Arab-Muslim country to recognize an Islamist political party. No political party, no association, no international organization had ever opposed it.

On September 27, Ahmed Ben Bella, the first president of independent Algeria, who had been in exile since his release in 1980, returned home. He had meanwhile created the Movement for Democracy in Algeria (MDA) in May 1985, which was legalized on December 15, 1989. Ait Ahmed, leader of the FFS, also returned to Algeria after 23 years in exile, and especially after the legalization of his party on November 20, 1989. Mahfoudh Nahnah, for his part, initially confined himself to the charitable association "*El Islah ouel Irchad*", created on November 30, 1989. A year later, he took the plunge and set up his own political party, the current Hamas[46].

The June 1990 elections and the Gulf War

The 1989-1990 social year, coinciding with the appointment of Mouloud Hamrouche as head of government and the legalization of certain political parties, was marked by unprecedented political unrest. The street became a political battleground. Each party tried to win over the population. Meetings, conference-debates and rallies followed one

---

46. According to Hichem Aboud (*La Mafia des généraux*, Lattès, 2002), Mahfoudh Nahnah's party was set up in the office of General Betchine, head of the secret services at the time.

another, with a certain advantage for those who already had a popular base and an underground organization, such as the FIS, the FFS, the MDA, the Parti d'Avant-Garde Socialiste (PAGS), or the FLN which, as the party in power, benefited from all the state logistics and propaganda resources.

And so the Algerian people, deprived of expression for almost thirty years, discovered freedom of speech and went to drink it in. Algerians discussed politics in factories, colleges, markets, public transport and stadiums. Groups of young and not-so-young discussed the world for hours on end at the foot of buildings. The university had become the primary place of political expression for almost all parties, with the exception of the FIS. Some situations were unusual: dignitaries of the Algerian regime found themselves obliged to explain their previous attitudes to academics, and each of their lectures became an examination paper in which the academic was the marker.

One of the first decisions taken after the 1992 coup d'état was to ban politics from universities. A political conscience was emerging, but it was very disturbing for certain business-minded decision-makers lacking in intellectual baggage. Mouloud Hamrouche's government was also disturbing. His attempt to reform the economy, bring greater transparency to the management of business and put an end to certain monopolies was to displease all the rentiers of the regime and incur their wrath.

The first decision taken, which upset some business-minded military personnel, was to reform the composition of the commission responsible for distributing contracts. The commission, which for years had been made up of six military members and three civilians, was recomposed to limit the influence of the military in business: only five civilians and two military members. The latter would never forgive Mouloud Hamrouche for this gesture, and took advantage of the FIS strike in June 1991 to get rid of him; they would later try to blame him for the tragedy that followed, on the grounds that the FIS had been legalized. But nobody was fooled. In 1999, another Islamist party was legalized.

As part of his anti-corruption drive, Mouloud Hamrouche created a system for controlling the acquisition of contracts in Algeria, particularly in the hydrocarbons sector, where the rent had become the raison d'être of these corrupt men. When Mouloud Hamrouche was appointed Prime Minister by Chadli Bendjeddid, he believed he was capable of leading the country out of crisis and, above all, negotiating honourably with the International Monetary Fund (IMF). Indeed, at the time of his appointment in September 1989, over 65% of exports would be swallowed up by foreign debt, making it impossible for the State to finance imports. But the IMF wanted to impose its vision of the economy on Algeria, and discussions with the government were shrouded in the utmost secrecy.

Against this difficult backdrop, Mouloud Hamrouche's government came in for criticism from a number of political parties. This meant that every conceivable thesis or theory could be considered, as long as there was partisan consumption.

It was against this economic backdrop that the first political demonstrations took place. Demonstrations of strength by occupying the streets gave an idea of the mobilization capacity of each political tendency. On Thursday April 19, 1990, a so-called democratic coalition marched through the streets of Algiers to celebrate the "Berber Spring", making this demand a *sine qua non* for the realization of democratic and cultural freedoms in Algeria. The march, in which the PAGS (former Communist Party) and the RCD (Rassemblement pour la Culture et la Démocratie) took part, failed to attract large crowds, despite the mobilization of a large section of the press. The indifference shown by the people of Algiers towards this demonstration was striking, and did not escape the attention of the special envoys of the international press. The following day, the FIS also organized a march from the Place du 1er-Mai to the presidential palace, its unavowed aim being to show international opinion its capacity for mobilization. The march was the first plebiscite for Abassi Madani's party. It drew hundreds of thousands of demonstrators, according to Islamist militants, and fifty thousand according to the police. The FIS had shown that it should be taken into account in the future.

Abassi Madani was received at the presidency by an advisor to the president, to whom he handed a letter. The following day, rumors circulated in Algiers that Abassi

Madani had been received by the presidential chef... Imagine the state of mind!

On April 21, some media outlets were talking about the Iranization of the Algerian street. A month later, the electoral campaign began for the first free elections in independent Algeria: the elections for the communal and departmental assemblies (APC and APW). These elections took place on June 12, 1990. The FIS won over eight hundred communes, with more than four million votes (54.3% of voters), while the PAGS obtained around twenty thousand votes. The RCD, alone in Kabylia where it had a majority presence, benefited from the FFS boycott, and had to cede some communes to other political parties, including the FIS. The FFS and the MDA decided to boycott the elections, as a punishment for the FLN system.

On the same day, Abassi Madani warned the authorities against any attempt to question the election results. The day after the elections, a section of the press close to the secular movement denounced the birth of an Islamic Republic on Europe's doorstep. The security services then took action. To discredit the party, they activated their system of infiltrators at all levels, from members of the Advisory Council to ordinary militants.

The success of the FIS in the communal elections was the result of a combination of factors: a sanction vote against the FLN party, a network of the population through a system of very active charitable associations, the use of mosques as a political forum, and a highly populist political discourse, a morbid game on the part of the regime, with a law on political associations aimed at fragmenting political representation, which led to the creation of some sixty empty shells, and the absence of any political alternative to the FLN (apart from self-proclaimed democratic groupings with surrealist discourse in a bloodless country, with a people whose memory is fractured and in search of an identity).

The management of the communes by the FIS, in which part of the Algerian people had placed their trust, did not differ fundamentally from that of the FLN. While there was certainly an aim to moralize politics within the governing bodies, at local level, the awarding of contracts and the distribution of social housing were not immune to graft and personal enrichment.

After the FIS plebiscite, Larbi Belkheir advised Chadli Bendjeddid to hand over his position as Minister of Defense to General Nezzar, so that he would not be directly involved in any possible showdown with FIS militants. Chadli Bendjeddid appointed General Nezzar to this post on June 25, and Toufik to replace Betchine as head of the DRS in September 1990, in order to prevent any temptation from Nezzar, and above all to separate the members of a duo that could become very troublesome: General Nezzar and General Betchine had collaborated in the repression of the events of October 1988. In addition, General Mediene had already made a name for himself at the head of the DCSA by preparing compromising files on a number of personalities. One of these files, frequently cited, is that of Riad El Feth.

Faced with this appointment, Belkheir saved Smaïn Lamari from certain retirement. He promoted him to the rank of colonel through Chadli Bendjeddid, after Betchine had accused him of connivance with the French secret services and sidelined him. Over the next decade, General Smaïn Lamari was to become the most feared man in Algeria. His arrival at the head of the Direction du Contre-Espionnage (DCE) was initially intended to prevent any alliance between Toufik and Nezzar. Over the years, he became the man who blew hot and cold both inside and outside the country. Among other things, he created the notorious "death squads", better known by their code name 192 (in reference to January 1st, 1992, the year of the coup d'état[47]). Their members were called "*Firka Saoutia*" ("musical group"), in allusion to their love of music during torture sessions: General Lamari's men would be cited in the "disappeared" affair (testimony of Abdelkader Tigha[48], former DRS brigade commander), in the assassination of senior army officers who had opposed certain decisions taken by their superiors (testimony of ex-colonel Samraoui), in the Paris attacks...

A few weeks after the FIS tidal wave, another event unexpectedly shook the international political scene in general, and the national scene in particular: the invasion

---

47. Habib Souaïdia, *op. cit.* p. 494.
48. www.algeria-watch.de/fr/article/pol/anp-présidence/dossier-politique.htm

of Kuwait, a sovereign state, by the despot in Baghdad. Claiming historical legitimacy for his rights to this land, in defiance of all international treaties and violating the UN Charter, and believing in his impunity for supposed services rendered to the West during the war against Iran, the Iraqi dictator offered the Americans and their allies an unhoped-for opportunity to reduce his military potential, and enabled a redistribution of the geopolitical map of the region following the collapse of the Soviet Union.

The day after the invasion, the official Arab world unanimously condemned Saddam Hussein. Considered for a time as the last bastion against the expansionism of the Iranian Islamic revolution, and as the saviour of the corrupt feudal monarchies of the Persian Gulf, Saddam Hussein was dropped. In the face of this hypocritical stance by Arab regimes, which followed the legitimate line of Western nations to respect the sovereignty of states, the street responded with marches by hundreds of thousands of people across almost all Arab countries, in support of the Iraqi people. At first, the Algerian authorities fell into a silence worthy of the Ice Age, but then, faced with international pressure, they were obliged to take a stand: they denounced the occupation of Kuwait and called on Iraq to withdraw and comply with international law. But the Algerian street, through popular mobilization, forced its leaders not to participate in the international coalition.

A few days before the outbreak of hostilities, Chadli Bendjeddid even toured the Middle East, meeting Saddam

Hussein, Iranian President Rafsadjani and Saudi King Fahd, among others, to urge them to find a peaceful solution to the crisis, but to no avail. At the same time, thousands of young Algerians recruited by the FIS landed in Amman via Tunis to join the front alongside the Iraqi army, led by two "DRS preachers", Ali Aya and Hachemi Sahnouni. These young recruits remained confined to highly guarded Iraqi barracks. They were even forbidden to leave the country, before being kindly escorted back to the border without having taken part in the war. For many observers, this was the first faux-pas committed by the FIS leadership, enabling the security services to identify all militants likely to represent a danger to public order. DRS agents simply collected the boarding cards of Islamist militants bound for Amman from their Tunisian counterparts[49]. However, this complacency on the part of the Algerian authorities was premeditated. At the right moment, it was necessary to convince Western opinion of the internationalist nature of this party.

Moreover, the FIS, by taking this surprising stand against the Gulf monarchies for a secular dictatorship, cut itself off from a certain financial windfall received through their powerful charities. The choice of the two preachers was not accidental. Ali Aya and Hachemi Sahnouni were known for their virulent preaching against those in power. Ali Aya was the man who, during the march organized by the FIS

---

49. Habib Souaïdia, *op. cit.* p. 235.

in support of the Iraqi people, declared in front of tens of thousands of demonstrators that the army only knew how to use its ammunition to kill its children. After 1992, this man was never bothered by the security services, apart from a short two-month stay in Reggane, where he was used as an intelligence agent (during this demonstration, Ali Benhadj, in military garb, and Abassi Madani were received at the government palace by General Nezzar and Mouloud Hamrouche, from whom they requested authorization to train their troops in barracks, which was refused).

As for Sahnouni, the key man of the services, he is quite simply the preacher of the famous mosque that General Nezzar is so fond of quoting, that of Kaboul in Belcourt. Not only was this founding member of the FIS never questioned, but throughout these ten years of "dirty war" he was the man Algerians rediscovered at every unfortunate opportunity. His background is as obscure as that of most of the founders of the FIS. He made a name for himself in the late 1980s: from his perch in Belcourt, he was renowned for his virulent and insulting preaching against those in power, whom he regarded as godless. During the events of October, he offered his mosque to Ali Benhadj so that he could challenge the army (Ali Benhadj was planning to call for a march in defiance of the state of siege, but some League members wisely persuaded him not to). After the creation of the FIS, Sahnouni became not only the guide, but also the spiritual leader of the radical FIS tendency, made up of the famous "Afghans". During the heyday of the FIS, this tendency formed the famous Islamic police force known as *"Djamâat amr bimaarouf oua nahy ala mounker"* ("Group that preaches the good and opposes the illicit"). This group could only act under the direct orders of the supreme leader. It was most of the militants in this group who made the trip to Iraq, to take part in the war. A few days after their return, and frustrated at not having taken on the Americans, they came close to clashing with the Republican Guard in the Mohammadia horse-riding center affair, following a virulent preaching by Sahnouni at the local mosque.

Without the intervention of Abassi Madani, who preferred to take legal action, the blood of the innocent would certainly have been shed. This group was later to become the GIA.

Some witnesses reported that the coup had been staged by the security services in order to make General Dib, head of the Republican Guard, aware of the danger posed by the FIS. But General Dib seemed unconcerned. The facts proved these witnesses right: before the coup, Chadli Bendjeddid called on General Dib to block General Nezzar's path[50]. He refused the offer, preferring to side with the Minister of Defense, at the President's expense.

---

50. Hichem Aboud, *op. cit.* p. 147.

The False Democratization Process and the Second Algerian War (1989-2007)

After the Gulf War, national politics took over again. Mouloud Hamrouche's government presented a draft for a new electoral map and a new electoral law, designed to benefit the FLN, the former single party.

The first opposition to the draft came from the late Kasdi Merbah, president of the Mouvement Algérien pour la Jeunesse Démocratique (MAJD party). The former head of Military Security criticized the draft for allowing the same people to remain in power. A few days later, Saïd Saadi, leader of the RCD, also voiced his opposition to the draft law.

Then, just before his appearance before the assembly, Abassi Madani broke his silence and threatened the authorities with a nationwide general strike, should such a draft be adopted by the FLN pseudo-parliament. The latter turned a deaf ear to this threat, and on April 1st, 1991, the bill was adopted by an overwhelming majority. The following day, in a communiqué signed by Abassi Madani, the FIS called on the President to intervene and cancel the bill, or "take responsibility for the disastrous consequences that could ensue". The following Friday, in his preaching at the Kouba mosque, Abassi Madani called on his militants to mobilize in the face of this new challenge from the powers that be.

In the face of almost total silence from all the political protagonists (with the exception of the Front des Forces Socialistes and the Parti des Travailleurs, who denounced the law), the FIS found itself increasingly engaged in an arm wrestling match with the authorities.

A month and a half later, the FIS Consultative Council, in the absence of Ali Benhadj who was touring the west of the country, called a general strike. Ali Benhadj was only informed of the strike decision the following day, by ordinary militants, as he was about to hold a meeting in Mascara. No member of the council, not even those closest to him, had informed him of the decision. Most of those who approved the decision remained untroubled by the events that followed.

Once back in Algiers, Ali Benhadj had several altercations with members of the council, and from that day on, he imposed his signature alongside that of Abassi Madani on all official FIS communiqués.

The day before the strike, Abassi Madani met Kasdi Merbah at a house near Kouba. In the course of their discussion, Kasdi Merbah warned Abassi Madani against certain members of the FIS council who might play a nasty trick on him. He advised him to call on the intellectual mass of the FIS to face up to the infiltrated elements of the Salafist majority.

At the same time, some members of the FIS consultative council and DRS agents were drawing up electoral lists, hoping for the failure of the strike, which would subsequently limit Abassi Madani's power. Candidatures were validated only after Sahnouni's guarantee.

On May 24, during a Friday sermon at the Mohammadia mosque, Abassi Madani called for a general strike until the FIS's demands, namely the annulment of all newly adopted texts, were fully met. As a result of the strike, the FIS discourse became more radical, going so far as to call for early presidential elections. Saturday May 25, 1991 was a "day without" for the FIS.

Most of the strikers were activists who had prepared a medical prescription to justify their work stoppage. The street seemed to be waiting to see. Even the Afghans didn't join in: Sahnouni hadn't given the order.

Apart from a few gatherings of dozens of people in front of the FIS headquarters in Algiers, in the Sunna, Belcourt or Kouba mosques, the strike went almost unnoticed on its first day. The first spark came from the hand extended by the Djazarists to Abassi Madani, from the universities in the center of the country, where, on the second day of the strike, a student mobilization had begun to take shape.

Following the gathering of students, whose shouts and slogans in favor of the FIS could be heard from the central faculty of Algiers, the FIS militants who were at the party headquarters moved to the outer enclosure of the faculty to express their support. The first lorries of CNS (France's equivalent of the CRS) soon arrived, prompting some young unemployed Algerians to join the demonstrators, given the bad memories left by the CNS during the events of October 1988. So the protest began and the strike took shape. That same evening, Abassi Madani called on his militants to stay on the streets and occupy public squares to ensure that the demonstrations did not lose momentum. Place du 1er-Mai and Place des Martyrs were the first to be occupied.

FIS militants were becoming increasingly organized, and every day the protest movement gained momentum. Young "hittists" were taking pleasure in shouting out their weariness of this two-faced system. The capital was increasingly paralyzed, but no real confrontation between FIS militants and the forces of law and order had taken place. Even the "Afghans" with their provocative slogans ("*dawla islamiya bla ma n'voto*": "Islamic State without a vote") didn't ignite the flames. The first tear gas canisters were not used until the fourth day of the strike, at Bab Ezzouar University, when students organized a ten-kilometer march in support of the FIS. Likewise, the following day, a tear-gas dispersal took place in Algiers to clear a path for motorists blocked by demonstrators.

On the same day, Abassi Madani declared that 90% of the workers in the Saharan gas and oil sectors were on strike, while there were rumors of large numbers of parachutists landing at Algiers and Boufarik airports. At the same time, General Nezzar appointed Generals Djouadi, Derradji, Touati and Taghrirt to draft a state of siege decree and a document establishing an advisory council to the President[51].

In this way, the army could keep an eye on politicians and control the decision-making spheres. This did not

---

51. Khaled Nezzar, *Mémoires du général Nezzar*, p. 215.

The False Democratization Process and the Second Algerian War (1989-2007)

come as a surprise to many Algerian specialists, for in fact, in December 1990, when Defense Minister Nezzar had appointed Touati, Lamari and Taghrirt as advisors to the Minister of Defense, he had already drawn up a "general staff"-type request[52], in case the FIS had exceeded the military's forecasts and probabilities, and had then escaped any external or internal control. So this "intelligentsia" had devised a multi-pronged strategy to ensure that the generals could never lose control of power. By all means, even illegal ones (electoral fraud, manipulation of public opinion), it was necessary to create the conditions for electoral success for any party that did not challenge the interests of the generals. At the same time, the so-called "hostile" parties, whether Islamist or not, had to be neutralized by legal means before the elections. Exploiting their antagonisms was a necessity. The birth of Sheikh Nahnah's Islamist party Hamas in December 1990 was part of this strategy. Hichem Aboud reports in his testimony[53] that on the eve of the party's creation, he saw Mahfoudh Nahnah leave the office of General Betchine, then head of Military Security.

On June 2, 1990, thousands of students demonstrated from the seafront to the Place des Martyrs in support of the FIS, despite the police cordon and the use of tear gas canisters.

---

52. Khaled Nezzar, *Échec à une régression programmée*, p. 148.
53. Hichem Aboud, *op. cit.* p. 94.

That same night, Mouloud Hamrouche and his government were deposed, and elite gendarmerie and police troops forcibly evacuated FIS militants from public squares. The toll was heavy: eighty dead according to NGOs, thirteen dead and sixty injured according to the police.

On June 4, a state of siege was declared. Sid Ahmed Ghozali was co-opted as head of government in place of Mouloud Hamrouche. It was necessary to eliminate the man of the reforms, a character judged not to be docile, and replace him with an executor of dirty deeds. The generals wanted to secure their financial interests (in 1994, when Algeria was in default, their foreign assets were estimated at around $34 billion, including $17 billion in France).[54]

On June 7, Abassi Madani announced the end of the strike, following an agreement he had allegedly reached with the head of government, Sid Ahmed Ghozali, but which the latter denied. According to the FIS leader, the agreement stipulated that the Islamist party would put an end to the strike and hostilities if the government responded favorably to three points: the repeal of the texts on electoral division and the electoral law, respect for the results of future legislative elections and the organization of an early presidential election. Seeing nothing coming, the FIS once again called for a general strike and, on June 15, 1991, asked its militants to reoccupy the streets. It was against this backdrop that the

54. Ali Yahia Abdenour, *Algérie, raisons et déraisons d'une guerre*, L'Harmattan, 2000, p. 142.

The False Democratization Process and the Second Algerian War (1989-2007)

first maquis formed around a number of radical Islamist figures: Chekendi at Chréa in the Mitidja, Mekhloufi at Zbarbar, as well as Chebouti and Meliani (charged in the Bouyali affair, then pardoned by Bendjeddid in 1989, and whose release Samraoui reports as part of an agreement with the security services to infiltrate and control the extremist tendency). Initially, they wanted to reactivate Bouyali's beloved Armed Islamic Movement (Mouvement Islamique Armé - MIA), but they went their separate ways after disagreement.

The generals' first attempt to implode the FIS was made through elements infiltrated into the Consultative Council. The aim was to definitively remove Abassi Madani and Ali Benhadj from the leadership of the party. To everyone's surprise, Algerian television showed a set of splittists calling on FIS militants to disobey Abassi Madani and Ali Benhadj's directives. On the set that day were Sahnouni (the preacher at the Belcourt mosque, who repeatedly threatened the authorities with jihad if they didn't apply Sharia law), Bachir Fkih (a preacher in Sidi Bel Abess, who died in an obscure manner a few days later on the road to Sidi Bel Abess, officially as the result of a road accident, and according to rumor as the result of an assassination) and Merani (a future minister and then senator). All were founding members of the FIS. During the broadcast, they denounced Abassi Madani's tyrannical nature, and accused him of being power-hungry, capable of sacrificing human lives to achieve his goals.

A few days later, a larger stage was organized. The speakers urged the demonstrators not to sacrifice themselves to Abassi Madani, but the street had already chosen its camp. Some of those who were on the TV set that day to denounce the violence of the FIS would take part in the first meeting for the creation of armed groups in Zbarbar on January 16, 1992.

Following this exclusive news from state television, Abassi Madani and Ali Benhadj organized a press conference on June 29, during which, in an excess of nervousness, they got to the bottom of their ideas. Ali Benhadj called for FIS militants' right to self-defense in the face of the generals' criminal nature. In the late afternoon, he was arrested at the headquarters of state television, along with other members of his entourage, when he went to demand a right of reply to the accusations made against him and Abassi Madani. The following morning, Madani was arrested in his turn at FIS headquarters. A campaign of arrests followed in Islamist circles. Over a thousand people were arrested, some of them extradited to concentration camps in the Algerian desert. In addition, over a hundred people were killed and more than a thousand wounded. General Nezzar's iron fist has once again brought mourning to Algerian families.

The December 1991 elections and the FIS victory

On June 26, 1991, Bendjeddid decided to hand over his post as president of the FLN to Abdelhamid Mehri, an early activist and former centralist with a moderate, dialogue-oriented tone. After the January 1992 coup d'état, Mehri established himself as a staunch opponent of the generals' eradicatory line and their relays in political circles and associations. This appointment enabled Chadli Bendjeddid to appear as the president of all Algerians, and to shed the cumbersome weight of a mastodon with feet of clay. The FLN party was hated by the population, and reforming it was illusory, given all the caciques reigning over it. Abdelhamid Mehri would learn this the hard way a few years later. So Bendjeddid put himself above the fray.

In the summer of 1991, the Prime Minister, Sid Ahmed Ghozali, brought together all the political parties (with the exception of the FIS) at the Club des Pins residence for a national conference. The debates were broadcast live on television. To make up for the absence of Abassi Madani's party, Sid Ahmed Ghozali made a number of dissidents, such as Kerrar and Merrani, his guests of honor, but they met with fierce opposition from certain parties who were unwilling to endorse the government's tactic of offering its dissident agents a platform to represent a party after having decapitated its legitimate leadership. Among these opponents, Louisa Hanoune, leader of the Parti des Travailleurs (Workers' Party), argued forcefully that these splittists should not take part in the debate or speak on behalf of a party whose militants accused them of treason.

Thus, after the arrest of the two historic FIS leaders on July 2, 1991, Mohamed Saïd and Abdelkader Hachani proclaimed themselves the sole legitimate spokesmen for the FIS, referring to a handover of instructions established by Abassi Madani before his arrest. On Friday July 5, in a virulent preaching, Mohamed Saïd attacked the authorities and called for the release of imprisoned leaders. He declared that the party would survive all the hardships it would face, and that it would continue on the path it had set out on.

Two days later, on July 7, following a meeting of the wilaya offices, a provisional executive board was appointed. Abdelkader Hachani was appointed president of this executive board, and Mohamed Saïd spokesman for the FIS. Just as he was about to give a press conference to explain the results of the proceedings, he was arrested in front of journalists. This arrest had no repercussions on the FIS congress, the date of which had just been set at a meeting of the wilaya offices.

On July 25 and 26, 1991, the first FIS congress was held in Batna, during which all dissidents were excluded. The delegates expressed their attachment to the historic leadership, and distanced themselves from any armed struggle in which some founding members had already embarked. Thus, in July 1991, Kamradinne Kerabane and Saïd Mekhloufi, both founding members of the FIS and former army officers, set up an armed group called *"El baqoune ala el ahd"* ("Faithful to the oath") at a meeting in the Zbarbar mountains. But after the coup d'état, Saïd Mekhloufi set up his own group, called MEI.

Immediately after the events of June 1991, the security services launched their first hunt for Islamists. The hunt targeted certain individuals considered dangerous, most of them former Bouyalists: Chebouti, Meliani, Hattab Abderahmane, Azzedine Bàa. But other individuals, unknown at the time, were also wanted: Moh Leveilly, Djaafer El Afghani and Yahia "Rougi". The latter group had found refuge and support in the Chakendi group at Tala Aicha in Chréa, already wanted by the security services since 1989. A new emir, Toufik, was chosen, while Chakendi was appointed military instructor. But in July, Toufik died in dubious circumstances and Chakendi temporarily became the group's emir, before being ousted at the end of July by Sahnouni's supporters.

During my stay in the Blida military prison alongside some of these people, I heard that it was then that Sahnouni took over the group. He became a spiritual guide, and convinced Meliani to join him. He later appointed him first emir. A year later, this group gave birth to the Groupe Islamique Armé. At the beginning of October 1991, two government newspapers, *El Massa* and *El Khabar*, carried an interview with Saïd Mekhloufi in which he explained the reasons that had led him to join the jihad against the regime.

On October 15, Chadli Bendjeddid announced legislative elections for the end of the year. A few days earlier, on September 30, the dinar had been devalued by 22%. At the same time, the law on hydrocarbon prospecting, research and pipeline transport activities was passed, following a visit by Algerians to IMF headquarters on September 2, to negotiate the terms and conditions of the April agreement under which the French BNP was charged with piloting a debt profiling program on Algeria's behalf, to the tune of one and a half billion dollars. This agreement had been signed by the former head of government, Mouloud Hamrouche, but his successor, Sid Ahmed Ghozali, called it into question. This explains the visit of IMF President Camdessus to Algiers on July 27, 1991[55]. Sid Ahmed Ghozali executed the terms of this agreement in a clumsy manner, raising suspicions, as analyst F. Rouzeir pointed out. The question remains: was the whole tragic summer of 1991 experienced by the Algerians not due to this?

On November 1st, 1991, the FIS rallied over five hundred thousand people in a march to celebrate the national holiday, making the release of its leaders a condition for its participation in the elections. On November 28, Mohamed Saïd was released provisionally by the prosecutor of the Blida military court. The following day, an armed group led by a certain Tayeb Afghani attacked the Guemmar barracks. A few days later, General Nezzar openly accused the FIS of being behind the attack. He unleashed his elite troops on the town of Guemmar, where atrocities were committed against the population, whose only fault was to have elected a FIS mayor.

At the trial between General Nezzar and Second-Lieutenant Souaïdia in Paris in July 2002, Captain Chouchene, a former Special Forces officer, gave a detailed

---

55. *Annuaire de l'Afrique du Nord (1991)*, p. 614.

and accurate account of the atrocities. Senior officers covered up the facts, believing that the local population deserved to be punished. The names of the criminals are known, as Captain Chouchene mentioned them at the trial.

On December 14, during a rally, Abdelkader Hachani announced the FIS's participation in the December 26 legislative elections, without referring to the presidential election. At his last meeting, held at the July 5 stadium in Algiers in front of over 100,000 militants, he urged the army and the President to respect the people's choice.

On December 26, 1991, the FIS won the legislative elections with more than 188 seats in the first round, ahead of the FFS (25 seats), and the heavily defeated FLN, the former single party (16 seats). For the second round, the FIS was in a dead heat in 167 constituencies, the majority of which were in a favorable position. These results caused an earthquake: those who had not voted for the FIS woke up with a hangover: panic swept through the Generals and their many relays in civil society. Some media launched a campaign to discredit the Islamist party that bordered on hysteria.

Western chancelleries got in on the act. A few days after the elections, the United States accused Algeria of possessing an atomic bomb and unconventional missiles. They demanded an inspection of the country's nuclear sites. But after the elections were interrupted in January 1992, the Americans announced that Algeria was not a nuclear power, and that its sites complied with international treaties, which left the Algerian street perplexed and led some of the population to say that the atomic bomb's name was "FIS".

After the elections won by the FIS, Algeria was to experience the greatest nightmare of its young history: it was to plunge into a civil war provoked by a military coup d'état led by a gang of unscrupulous generals, representing only themselves, aided by their henchmen and a host of parasites whose interests were linked to these corrupt individuals. They made the Algerian people pay a heavy price: two hundred thousand dead, tens of billions of dollars in material damage, thousands of missing persons, the deportation of tens of thousands of people to concentration camps in the middle of the desert, the torture of tens of thousands of people, the extrajudicial executions of thousands more, the creation of armed militias spreading terror, the creation of the GIA which committed crimes whose atrocity and ferocity are without equal in the history of humanity.

2. THE SECOND ALGERIAN WAR, THE BLACK DECADE

After the collapse of oil prices in 1986, and the negative growth recorded in 1986 (-1.6%), 1987 (-1.4%) and 1988 (-2.7%), combined above all with a population growth rate of around 3%, Algeria embarked on political reforms that put an end to the hegemony of the FLN single party.

Civil society regained its autonomy thanks to the 1989 Constitution, which recognized a multi-party system, and economic reforms were launched. Algeria had to negotiate structural adjustment with the IMF, aligning the dinar with its real value, which was close to that of the parallel market, and liberalizing foreign trade.

But in December 1991, the FIS won the legislative elections, and had promised during its campaign to rise up against the IMF diktat, saying that the Algerian debt was in Western bank accounts, where it had to be collected. This, at least in part, enabled the Algerian Generals to find justification with the world's big money-makers to liquidate this party, which threatened not only their interests, but also those of their foreign partners. It is only in this light that we can understand the lack of condemnation of the coup d'état, but also the concrete help the Algerian regime received to finance its war. Democracy has never existed to save Algeria, and the Islamist danger is a creation of those in power. Safeguarding the Republic by cancelling the elections is a mirage that can be lived with when interests are preserved. This party, tempted as it was to amend the Constitution, had other ways of avoiding the worst. It had lost a million votes in the year between elections, and Chadli Bendjeddid had the means, by virtue of his constitutional prerogatives, to dissolve Parliament if the Constitution was threatened. There were hundreds of appeals against FIS elected representatives, and almost half the Algerian population did not vote in the first round.

Fifteen days for a coup d'état

At 1 a.m. on December 27, Larbi Belkheir, Minister of the Interior since October 1991, announced the victory of the FIS. The same day, the government met. Aboubakr Belkaid, Minister of Justice, declared: "The problem is to know whether or not we should organize the second round[56]." Belkheir then took the floor and asserted that "Chadli [should] resign[57]". After the meeting, Sid Ahmed Ghozali asked General Nezzar to meet Bendjeddid to find out what he thought: he detected no panic on the part of the President, who considered this to be the law of the democratic game. But Nezzar understood that the President was in shock[58], which prompted him to meet FFS leader Ait Ahmed. Ait Ahmed asked him not to involve the army and to leave the matter to the politicians.

On the same day, General Nezzar set up what he called a "working and reflection group" at the Ministry of Defense, a kind of black cabinet, as well as a commission made up of ministers Ali Haroun and Aboubakr Belkaid, and generals Touati and Taghrirt, to find a legal framework for ending the crisis[59]. This commission represented a kind of second black cabinet, which would later serve as justification and cover for the real black cabinet installed the day before,

---

56. Hassane Zerrouky, *La Nébuleuse islamiste en France et en Algérie*, Éditions n° 1, 2002, p. 50.
57. *Le Matin*, January 10, 2002.
58. *Ibid.*
59. Khaled Nezzar, *Mémoires du général Nezzar*, p. 238; and Habib Souaïdia, *op. cit.*, p. 109.

The False Democratization Process and the Second Algerian War (1989-2007)

which was composed entirely of military personnel, already prepared for the idea of a coup d'état.

On December 29, Miloud Brahimi, a lawyer for the government and the military, contacted Abdelhak Benhamouda, head of the Union Générale des Travailleurs Algériens (UGTA) trade union, to launch a protest movement to block the FIS. On the same day, the Constitutional Council received appeals from the parties. The next day, the Prime Minister, Sid Ahmed Ghozali, declared that the elections had been clean, so as not to attract the attention of the President, since the mechanisms required for a coup de force were not yet ready. How else can we explain his subsequent about-turn on the question of the cleanliness of the elections?

On December 30[60], the Conseil National pour la Sauvegarde de l'Algérie (CNSA) took shape on the steps of the UGTA union headquarters, in front of two hundred people claiming to represent civil society. Numerous organizations and Miloud Brahimi's human rights league took part in the demonstration.

On December 31[61], the CNSA received the support of a number of parties that had been disavowed by the ballot box (Saïd Saadi's RCD, Kasdi Merbah's MAJD and Hachemi Cherif's PAGS, a former Communist Party) in the hope of a rebirth under the bayonets. The PAGS did not even take part

---

60. *Le Matin*, January 10, 2002.
61. Abed Charef, *Algérie, le grand dérapage*, Éditions de l'Aube, 1995, p. 244.

in the legislative elections. The CNSA was also supported by a number of intellectuals, artists and former ministers.

The FFS called on Algerians to demonstrate on January 2, 1992 in Algiers. It called for citizen mobilization for the second round and believed it could win over the abstentionists from the first round. However, the military used the demonstration as an argument for their approach, even though it was only organized for electoral purposes. The CNSA decided to march under the slogans of the Front des Forces Socialistes, but only Ait Ahmed spoke on the day of the march[62]. Five hundred thousand people marched along the Algiers seafront under the slogan "Neither police state, nor fundamentalist state". Unfortunately, the march served as an alibi for the putschists.

That same evening, twenty-five high-ranking army officers gathered at Aïn Naadja, where Algeria's fate was sealed. The solution of a coup d'état was adopted, all that remained was to choose the form it would take. The meeting lasted all night. On January 3 itself, the FIS, having learned the news[63], requested an audience with the President through Hachani, acting president of an Islamist party. The President of the Republic and Supreme Commander of the Armed Forces was astonished by the news brought to him by Hachani. He was shocked to learn of such a meeting. Immediately after this meeting, Bendjeddid summoned General Nezzar,

---

62. Habib Souaïdia, *op. cit.* p. 375.
63. Hichem Aboud, *op. cit.* p. 146.

asking him to organize a meeting with senior army officers, scheduled for January 6.

On January 4, the President of the French National Assembly, Abdelaziz Belkhadem, organized an end-of-mandate ceremony for future former MPs from the single party[64]. During the ceremony, Belkhadem made no criticism whatsoever of the way in which the elections had been conducted.

The following day, on the eve of Chadli Bendjeddid's famous meeting with army officers, Sid Ahmed Ghozali, who had previously declared that the ballot had not been marred by any irregularities, went back on his word, deeming that the ballot had not been honest[65]. Some would say that this was the lifeline that saved General Nezzar the next day from certain impeachment, which the President wanted in front of all the officers in order to regain control of the army.

But in the face of this media outcry, Bendjeddid was content to say, during the meeting on January 6, and after hearing everyone, that he would take the necessary decisions. On January 7 and 8, he met Belkhadem[66] in his capacity as President of the National Assembly. Belkhadem later said that Chadli Bendjeddid had never informed him of the end of his mission. On January 8, the President received FLN leader Abdelhamid Mehri, to whom he said

---

64. *Le Matin*, January 10, 2002.
65. Reporters sans frontières, *op. cit.* p. 143.
66. Belkhadem's testimony at the trial of FIS leaders in 1992.

nothing about his probable resignation. He also received Abdelkader Hachani, who assured him that he would never call for early presidential elections if the second round of legislative elections were held, and promised to govern within the framework of the Constitution.

On Thursday January 9, Chadli Bendjeddid received a man he greatly respected, General Djenouhat, in the company of General Nezzar. The President felt secure in the words of the Minister of Defense. After this meeting, he retired to spend the weekend in Zeralda, in complete tranquillity. On the same day, rumours abounded that an impressive number of military personnel would be landing at the Boufarik and Algiers bases.

The FIS leadership met clandestinely that evening, preparing for an increasingly likely coup. Sid Ahmed Ghozali declared that "we must expect solutions". On January 10, while preaching at the Kouba mosque, Abdelkader Hachani declared that "the people should expect their choice to be confiscated". According to Hichem Aboud, Chadli Bendjeddid was not informed of the sound of the boots until the morning of Saturday January 11. Faced with this fait accompli, he informed General Dib, head of the Republican Guard, that he had just appointed him to head the army in place of General Nezzar, who was also subsequently informed. The countdown was thus on, even before we had a definitive answer from the luxury joker found over the weekend in Morocco: Mohamed Boudiaf.

Ali Haroun travelled to Kenitra on January 11 to convince him to at least come and talk to the military[67], which he did the following day. Still according to Hichem Aboud[68], Generals Lamari, Ghozeil, Dib and Nezzar entered the presidential offices on the morning of January 11, insulting and threatening Chadli Bendjeddid. The latter, cut off from his own bodyguards, abdicated and signed his resignation. But in his television statement that same evening, he said: "The only conclusion I have reached is that I cannot continue to exercise my duties to the full without failing the sacred oath I have made to the nation." Chadli Bendjeddid officially resigned, but never cancelled the election.

Boudiaf, from his arrival to his assassination

By precipitating the departure of Chadli Bendjeddid, the Generals and Nezzar found themselves faced with an unprecedented situation: a constitutional vacuum. In response, they convened a meeting of the High Security Council (HCS), chaired by Sid Ahmed Ghozali, even though the decree of October 24, 1989 stipulated that the HCS could only be chaired by the President, and included the President of the National Assembly, the Ministers of Defense, Foreign Affairs, the Interior, Justice and the Economy, as well as the Army Chief of Staff. Why, then,

---

67. Khaled Nezzar, *Mémoires du général Nezzar*, p. 253.
68. Hichem Aboud, *op. cit.* p. 147.

does a president who resigned of his own accord only the day before not hold a meeting of the HCS, and cancel the election himself? The HCS has decided to halt the electoral process[69]. For most Algerians, that day was fateful, sealing the fate of the people so that the interests of certain generals and their henchmen could be protected.

Ten years on, some of these people continue to enrich themselves illicitly. The anarchy that followed, encouraged by the weakness and illegitimacy of the government in power, terrorism in all its abject variants, opposition between groups of citizens, the criminal acts of the security services, and the vendetta of militiamen armed by the regime, led to the emergence of scourges that had previously existed little or not at all in Algerian society.

Crime figures rose at an alarming rate, prompting the authorities, a decade later, to make the fight against organized crime as much a priority as the fight against terrorism. Armed attacks on private and public property, and sometimes on anonymous citizens, increased. False roadblocks set up by real or fake Islamist terrorists (or real criminals in any case), or by terrorist or criminal police officers, have multiplied. Drug use, sometimes involving young children and women, took its toll: cocaine, heroin, psychotropic drugs, glue and other toxic substances were added to the traditional "kif". Misery and despair have driven often young women, sometimes teenagers, into prostitution.

---

69. *Le Matin*, January 10, 2002.

Boudiaf landed in Algiers on January 12, 1992 in the greatest secrecy[70]. He met with the army chiefs, who assured him of their full cooperation. In front of an audience of senior officers gathered at Aïn Naadja that same night, Boudiaf was sworn in that any decisions he took or actions he undertook would be respected. At the end of the meeting, he asked for a few more days to return to Morocco and settle his domestic affairs.

On January 13, at a meeting of FIS elected representatives, a crisis cell was set up, comprising Ikhlef Cherati, Mohamed Saïd, Kacem Tadjouri and Abderazak Redjam. Its role was to ensure the party's continuity in the underground, and to implement a new strategy to ensure its survival.

During the night of January 13 to 14, the FIS headquarters were emptied of all documentation and computer equipment. On the same day, FFS leader Ait Ahmed, who considered Bendjeddid's pseudo-demission and the HCS's decision to cancel the second round of legislative elections to be tantamount to a coup d'état, implored the FIS not to engage in the violence intended by the military, Abdelhamid Mehri, General Secretary of the FLN, met with Abdelkader Hachani and asked him to renounce violence in favor of dialogue.

Internationally, no country has issued an official condemnation. France, historically linked to Algeria, was in the know from the outset. The day after the first round of

---

70. Hichem Aboud, *op. cit.* p. 159.

legislative elections, Chadli Bendjeddid had informed the French ambassador in Algiers, Jean Audibert, of his intention to cohabit with the Islamists. The ambassador was also informed a few days later by General Larbi Belkheir of the Generals' intention to cancel the second round of these elections. This prompted François Mitterrand to send an emissary, the Arabist general Philippe Rondot[71], to Algiers in early January. He asked for the President's security to be guaranteed, and received assurances from the quarteron of putschists in Algiers that they would carry out their operation "with respect for human rights".

Former president Valéry Giscard d'Estaing and Jean-Marie Le Pen were the only French politicians to condemn the coup. François Mitterrand only distanced himself from the coup at the end of 1992, during a European summit chaired by France.

The Algerian Generals only survived thanks to support from Paris, where pressure was brought to bear on the Paris Club and other international institutions to help the putschists. The flow of money from European Economic Community (EEC) countries shortly after the coup is therefore easy to understand.

On January 14, a collegial leadership, known as the Haut Comité d'État (HCE), was created to ensure the country's transition. The HCE was made up of Mohamed Boudiaf, Ali Haroun (Minister of Justice), Khaled Nezzar (Minister

----

71. www.algeria-watch.de/fr/article/analyse/lamine_eradiction.htm

of Defense), Tidjani Haddam (Rector of the Paris Mosque) and Ali Kafi (Secretary General of the organization of moudjahidines or veterans). The presidency of the HCE was granted to Boudiaf as a key player in the Algerian revolution. Boudiaf's return to Algeria after 27 years of exile in Morocco to collaborate with the putschists is one of the greatest enigmas of this period in Algeria's history. Only a year earlier, he had declared on Algerian television (invited by Ait Ahmed and Ben Bella to return home) that he had no confidence in the regime. How could he have been convinced in just two days, even with the help of friends and family? What did Ali Haroun promise him during his visit to Kenitra? What was in the letter he was given?

By answering all these questions, we might be able to explain why he agreed to act as a front for the Generals, and help Algerians understand the reasons behind his assassination.

On January 15, Abdelkader Hachani declared that Boudiaf was an imported president. The following day, Boudiaf officially returned to Algeria. He told the press that he had come to save Algeria, and that he was extending his hand to all Algerians without exception. Voices were raised to warn him that he was on the wrong track, and that he risked his life if he thought he was collaborating with the Generals. These voices were right: Boudiaf was the second president in the entire world to be assassinated live on television, on June 29, 1992.

On the very day of his arrival in Algiers, a meeting to unify the armed Islamist opposition was held in Zbarbar, attended by the radicals expelled from the FIS (Sahnouni, Zebda Benazouz, Saïd Mekhloufi) and the Bouyalists (Chebouti, Meliani). It was a non-committal contact meeting, but it did enable Meliani to find potential support for his ideas in Sahnouni and Zebda. At the end of the meeting, the group parted company and agreed to meet again in Sidi Moussa, to clarify matters further. During this second meeting, no consensus could be reached and each protagonist tried to prove his effectiveness on the ground, hence the start of the attacks.

Despite the denunciation of the stoppage of the electoral process by the three Fronts (FIS, FLN, FFS), the situation deteriorated day by day. On January 18, in front of a crowd of journalists, the FIS elected representatives were evacuated with batons by the police from the Comité Populaire de la Ville d'Alger (CPVA), where they were holding a meeting. That same evening, Abdelkader Hachani declared that his party had exhausted all legal avenues to prevent the country from going off the rails.

The following day, the security forces began making arrests in Islamist circles. The first people arrested were tortured simply because they belonged to the FIS. The FIS reacted with a communiqué signed by Abdelkader Hachani, warning the authorities against any excesses, and calling on the international community to assume its responsibilities. It also specified that it would not recognize any treaty or commitment drawn up by the new government, and warned the West against any collaboration with the new regime. The same evening, the HCE reacted in the press, describing the FIS leaders as destabilizers. The showdown then took shape, and the second Algerian war could begin.

On January 21, the mosque war broke out between the military, who considered that places of worship also served as propaganda grounds for FIS militants, and the latter, who considered that places of worship were the only places of freedom left to them.

The demonstrations were put down in bloodshed. The first urban clashes resulted in an impressive number of deaths and bullet wounds among FIS militants. Within days, hundreds of people were arrested and deported to concentration camps in the middle of the desert: Reggane was the first of these camps, officially opened in February 1992.

On January 22, Abdelkader Hachani was arrested because he had called on the military not to obey orders from their superiors and not to shoot at demonstrators. He spent five years in the notorious Serkadji prison. Once released, he was assassinated because of his opposition to the civil concord concocted by the Generals. A few days later, Rabah Kebir was also arrested, and released shortly afterwards for lack of charges by the judge, who was later transferred. He was placed under house arrest, but managed to leave the country clandestinely, heading for Germany.

February 1992 is the month that Algerians would like to erase from their memories and from the calendar. Indeed, although they had been accustomed since independence to excesses of violence between citizens and the forces of law and order, never before had the horror of these confrontations reached such limits. Human life no longer had any meaning in the eyes of those who held the power of arms: those who could kill killed; those who could humiliate humiliated; those who could rape raped... Unprecedented events erupted: six young policemen were killed on rue Bouzrina in Algiers, following an ambush by a group of armed Islamists. They were led by Kamel Brimer, a former member of the Islamic police (who later pledged allegiance to Mansouri Miliani, future leader of the GIA), and Abdelghani Abdelaoui, also a member of the Islamic police. The latter was arrested and convicted in connection with this case. He escaped from Lambese prison in March 1994 and became a close associate of GIA leaders Djamel Zitouni and Antar Zouabri.

Three days later[72], the officer in charge of the investigation found the machine-gun used in the attack in the well of a house in the Casbah: a stolen rifle from the Admiralty, never declared. Worse still, he discovered that some members of this group were members of the Algiers Admiralty's marine corps. After these soldiers had been arrested and brought before the judge, who sentenced them to death, a warrant

----

72. Mohamed Samraoui, *op. cit.* p. 147.

officer belonging to this group was spotted by police officers walking freely around Place des Martyrs.

On the civil protest front, the uprising in Batna, involving almost the entire population of the town, left its mark. The protests lasted four days, with fourteen people shot dead and one hundred and seventy injured, according to official figures. Following the protests on the central campuses, the security forces occupied almost all the central universities, arresting students inside the lecture halls.

On February 9, the HCE declared a state of emergency for one year, and Mohamed Boudiaf held a press conference at which he reported on the security situation, announcing a toll of fifty dead and two hundred wounded (one hundred and fifty dead and seven hundred wounded according to the FIS), following the army's campaign since January 21 to retake mosques. Two days later, Mohamed Boudiaf gave magistrates carte blanche to deal with corruption cases. At the same time, Italy granted the first major loan in support of the Generals' coup: three hundred million dollars to finance imports. A few days earlier, France had granted a loan of five hundred million dollars to the Algerian regime. And strangely enough, on February 13, in a televised communiqué, the Generals announced the creation of seven concentration camps in the middle of the Algerian desert, some of which were located on nuclear test sites, such as Reggane and Aïn M'Guel, and others which had been used for chemical testing, such as Oued Namous, Menaa, Ouargla, Aïn Salah and Bordj Omar Idriss. A few days later, Ali Haroun announced the arrest of five thousand people (fourteen thousand according to the FIS). The following day, a certain section of the press justified the arrests by citing the attack on the admiralty by an armed group the previous day, which had left six people dead[73].

On February 22, Saïd Guechi, a former FIS radical expelled from the party by Abdelkader Hachani at the Batna congress in July 1991, joined Sid Ahmed Ghozali's government as Minister of Employment. On March 2, while large numbers of people were being arrested and transferred to camps, the government announced the discovery of eight oil fields in southern Algeria. Naturally, the Generals played the oil card with regard to the West, in order to conceal all the atrocities committed. Thus, to scare Westerners with the thesis of Islamism on Europe's doorstep, the Tlemcen court handed down death sentences to three members of a group called Hezbollah.

Towards the end of the month, three major events marked the political scene in Algeria. Firstly, the FIS was dissolved by the Algiers administrative court. Then, two days later, the FIS appealed, and Kebir was acquitted for lack of charges. Finally, between these two events, on March 30, General Mohamed Lamari was retired by presidential decree[74] and was not replaced by General Khalifa Rahim until nineteen days after his dismissal. Khaled Nezzar took him

---

73. During the Algiers airport bombing trial, Mansouri Meliani claimed responsibility for the attack on the admiralty.
74. *Annuaire de l'Afrique du Nord (1992)*, p. 654.

back, appointing him advisor to the Minister of Defense. Ten years on, very few people speak of this event, or shed any light on the conflict between Mohamed Boudiaf and General Lamari.

On April 1st, Japan stepped in and granted Algeria a credit of three hundred million dollars. A week later, the International Bank for Research and Development (IBRD) released a loan of three hundred and fifty million dollars.

On April 9, Ahmed Merani, a former founding member of the FIS, was appointed advisor to the head of government on religious affairs, and later became a senator. On April 12, the Blida military court brought six charges against Ali Benhadj, and five against Abassi Madani, most of which carried the death penalty. On April 22, the National Consultative Council (CCN) was set up to fill the vacancy in Parliament: made up of sixty members appointed by the High State Committee (HCE), it brought together all the rapacious and opportunistic members of the regime, people with no past and no future, whose time in this institution will leave no more traces than those who preceded them. Reda Malek has been appointed by his friends as president of the most puppet-like body that has ever existed in our country.

On the same day, the IBRD granted another trade libe-ralization loan. Shortly afterwards, parasitic companies were set up to act as a front for the flight of Algerian assets abroad, under the name of "import-export companies". In response, seven political parties called on the government to form a government of national unity, lift the state of siege and close concentration camps. Ten years later, Mohamed Boudiaf's son told[75] that "the concentration camps were General Larbi Belkheir's idea, that his father was against them and that he wanted to put an end to them".

On April 28, General Bellouçif emerged as the first turkey in the fight against corruption and embezzlement: he was arrested and accused by his own people of embezzling state funds. He was imprisoned for three years, even though he had been sentenced to twelve years' imprisonment. In the meantime, Boudiaf was assassinated and replaced by Colonel Ali Kafi, who was himself dismissed and replaced by General Zeroual, who was later forced to resign. Justice had nothing to do with this affair, as with others: affairs are made and unmade according to alliances. Some of our current leaders live in palaces in the heart of Algiers, even though all their lives they have been civil servants. Not to mention all the wealth, visible or otherwise, accumulated by them or their offspring. Morals and ethics have given way to the law of the jungle.

At the beginning of May 1992, the Ouargla court ruled on the Guemmar case, after only three months of investigation - a record for criminal investigations, and above all for a terrorist act against state security. Thirteen death sentences were handed down.

---

75. *Le Matin*, January 10, 2002.

The False Democratization Process and the Second Algerian War (1989-2007)

Exactly one month later, Boudiaf was assassinated during a tour of the eastern part of the country, in the town of Annaba. None of the decision-makers were on the trip that day. General Larbi Belkheir, Minister of the Interior, General Toufik, head of the DRS, and his deputy, General Smaïn Lamari, head of counter-espionage, had all stayed behind, an insane thing for a trip where Mohamed Boudiaf was due to meet some twenty prefects (walis). He was assassinated by a man from the Groupe d'Intervention Spéciale (GIS), Lieutenant Boumarafi, who had been added to the list of escorts at the last minute. He magically found himself inside the conference enclosure, behind the curtains, whereas the mission of this kind of group is to secure the outside. Securing the interior is the responsibility of the president's bodyguards and military security. Mohamed Boudiaf was assassinated during a speech broadcast live on state television, the last word of which was "Islam". The presumed assassin gave himself up to the police, and the investigation was botched. The hypothesis of a plot was ruled out, even though witnesses claimed that the hypothesis of a second gunman with an attempted diversion was true. A replica of the John Fitzgerald Kennedy assassination? In May 2006, Boudiaf's wife, in a confession to the Qatari channel El-Djazira, referred to a videotape which clearly showed the assassination of her husband; she even spoke to Bouteflika about it to relaunch the investigation, but to no avail...

A few days before his death, Mohamed Boudiaf had ordered the arrest of the biggest smuggler in Algerian history, Hadj Bettou: he was arrested by a gendarmerie brigade specially dispatched from Algiers, commensurate with his influence over a large part of the South. He was brought before a military court, the Blida tribunal, where he was sentenced to only six months' imprisonment.

During my stay in this prison, I learned from some inmates who knew him that Hadj Bettou was illiterate and incapable of inspiring this kind of trafficking. How then could he manage one of the country's largest fortunes? Add to this the sense of tranquillity that inspired him: he felt in no way threatened, and behaved like a pasha, distributing balls, tracksuits and even dates to prisoners accused of acts of terrorism. A "loudmouth", he liked to boast about the number of Kalashnikovs that vanished between Boufarik airport and Blida. He was reportedly arrested with two hundred rifles[76]: this would explain why he was brought before a military court and prosecuted for possession and trafficking of weapons of war, whereas at the time of his arrest, he had been handed over to a civilian court. But once he was brought before the judge, he had only two rifles left. It is these two Kalashnikovs that General Nezzar refers to in his testimony about this affair, forgetting the essential point.

In reality, Hadj Bettou was simply Nezzar's henchman, as Hichem Aboud so aptly put it. The three officers, including a certain Commandant Mourad, who worked on the case

---

76. Hichem Aboud, *op. cit.* p. 191.

were assassinated[77]. Meanwhile, Mohamed Boudiaf had become close to Kasdi Merbah, whom he wanted to put back in charge of the secret services. General Mediene had even tried to prevent Boudiaf from attending his son's wedding in Kenitra, Morocco, as Kasdi Merbah had been invited.

In fact, after just a few months, Mohamed Boudiaf had made enemies of all the members of the "black cabinet": General Mohamed Lamari, whom he dismissed; General Nezzar, whose affairs he touched; Generals Mediene and Smaïn Lamari, who risked losing their posts with the return of Kasdi Merbah; and General Belkheir, through his handling of the FIS case. By expressing misgivings about the conclusions of the commission of inquiry set up to investigate the circumstances surrounding the death of Mohamed Boudiaf, Maître Fathallah, President of the Ligue des Droits de l'Homme (Human Rights League), signed his own death warrant: the GIA gunned him down a few days later.

However, a reading of the commission's report highlighted a series of anomalies, which, when accumulated, could not have been the result of chance, as an extract from the report testifies: "The fact remains that the shortcomings, negligence and carelessness that we noted at all levels of the services that programmed the visit, organized its conduct and ensured the President's security, were directly or indirectly the factors that objectively facilitated the execution." Thus, Lieutenant Boumarafi had a different

---

77. Mohamed Samraoui, *op. cit.* p. 156.

mission order from that of his colleagues in the same security corps, signed by Commander Hamou. Just after Mohamed Boudiaf's death, General Nezzar defended the latter, body and soul, at a meeting of senior army and secret service officers attended by Kamel Abderahmane, Toufik, Smaïn Lamari, Samraoui and Saïdi Fodhil. The latter was assassinated in 1996.

The gendarmes were not allowed to monitor the room, and their means of communication were jammed half an hour before the attack. The ambulance driver who transported Mohamed Boudiaf after the attack did not know his route, and the bodyguards had deserted their posts. No ballistic analysis or autopsy has been carried out. The bomb was found under the stage at El-Hadjar. The theory of the presence of several gunmen was dismissed, although it was justified by the bullet that hit Mohamed Boudiaf in the chest[78], by Boumaarafi's grenades[79] recovered during a sweep carried out by Smaïn Lamari's men, and by the presentation of the accused before a civilian court, whereas he was under court martial jurisdiction. The prosecutor in charge of the case was promoted to a consular post abroad... How can we speak of an isolated act when all this is taken into consideration? I leave it to the pseudo-democrats, those thirsting for military justice, and the defenders of the Generals to come up with an answer that will enlighten us. But I ask you to let the man who considered

---

78. Youcef Zirem, *Algérie, la guerre des ombres*, Éditions Complexe, 2002, p. 29.
79. Mohamed Samraoui, *op. cit.* p. 259.

them friends and brothers rest in peace, and to leave his memory untouched; the very people who pointed to him as their hope have betrayed him.

Another event that could be linked to Mohamed Boudiaf's death was the opening of the trial of the FIS leaders a few days later at the Blida military court. On July 15, 1992, after a three-day trial, Abassi Madani and Ali Benhadj were sentenced to twelve years in prison, while the other five leaders of the Islamist party received sentences ranging from four to six years.

Despite all the assurances given by the regime to the various authorities on the transparency of the trial for the assassination of Mohamed Boudiaf, it will be marred by irregularities and NGOs will not attend.

Escalation from Zbarbar to Algiers airport

After the first two meetings in January 1992, held on the Zbarbar and Sidi Moussa mountains, which were a semi-failure, all the leaders of the armed Islamist groups met for a third time on the Zbarbar mountains between late March and early April, at the time of Ramadan. The same people as at the first two meetings (Zebda, Sahnouni, Meliani, Chebouti, Mekhloufi) were present, as well as the leaders of groups operating in Algiers and its outskirts, including Moh Leveilly. The congressmen set up an armed struggle organization, the MIA, whose national emir was Chebouti, promoted to the rank of general. Mensouri Meliani became national coordinator of the struggle. Moh Leveilly, reduced to a secondary role, did not join the organization and left the meeting. Some time later, Mansouri Meliani relinquished his post as national coordinator to resume his position as group leader of the center. Together with Moh Leveilly, he tried to unify all the groups at the center. This work could not be completed, as Mansouri Meliani was arrested in August 1992, and Moh Leveilly shot dead in the same month. This work was completed by Layada Abdelhak, and gave rise to the Groupe Islamique Armé in September 1993.

The first act attributed to the MIA was the Algiers airport bombing at 10 a.m. on August 26, 1992. The airport was blown up by a bomb placed under the passenger seats in the central hall, resulting in a high-intensity explosion that killed nine people and injured around a hundred. The group accused of carrying out the attack was dismantled within a fortnight. All the participants were arrested: Hocine Abderahim, a former FIS elected representative in Bouzereah, Rachid Hchaichi, a captain on Air Algérie, and Soussene[80], who at the time of the attack was already under arrest (arrested on August 18, 1992, one week before the attack). There were no casualties among the members of the security services present at the scene. A rumour circulating among the traffickers reported that no customs or police officers (plainclothes or uniformed) were seen at this usually heavily watched and frequented location. The bomb was planted near the airport cafeteria, a popular

---

80. Reporters sans frontières, *op. cit.* p. 185.

place for airport police and customs officers to do business, and a meeting place for vultures and birds of prey attracted by the influx of immigrants during the summer months. If the courts are certain of the involvement of all these people in this attack, then anyone who has entered this terminal at least once in his or her life is certain that the security services, of all bodies, knew about it and let the bomb explode. On May 17, 1993, the Algiers court sentenced seven participants to death[81], executed on August 31, 1993 in Berrouaghia prison.

The GIA, Zeroual and oil

A week after Mohamed Boudiaf's death, BP, Philips petroleum, Mobil and Atlantic Richter obtained permits to exploit oil fields[82].

The day after the agreement was signed, Sid Ahmed Ghozali was replaced at the head of the government by Belaïd Abdeslam, former Minister of Industry under Boumediene, an old apparatchik who has decreed a war economy, as long as it doesn't affect him.

Ali Kafi, another regime insider and General Secretary of the Organisation Nationale des Moudjahidines (veterans of the Algerian War of Independence), replaced Mohamed Boudiaf at the head of the HCE, an empty shell since real power is in the hands of the military. When he was ousted

---

81. Among others, Hocine Abderahim, Rachid Hchaichi, Soussene and Mansouri Meliani.
82. *Annuaire de l'Afrique du Nord (1992)*, p. 656.

in favor of Zeroual, he refused to leave his state residence, as did Sid Ahmed Ghozali, in his capacity as Algerian ambassador to Paris, after having served as head of government. Reda Malek joined the High State Committee.

Mohamed Boudiaf's plan to create a large rally (Rassemblement National Patriotique) was blown up by clan conspiracies, to which the hands of the regime's dignitaries were no strangers. Meanwhile, Algeria was plunged into civil war and economic crisis (it had defaulted on its debts). At the time, it was going through an unprecedented economic crisis, despite being ranked eleventh among oil-producing countries, with 1.8% of world production, and sixth for gas, with 2.7% of world production and 4% of world reserves. The country was faced with debt repayment difficulties caused by the collapse in foreign currency earnings from oil, its only source of income, whose price had plummeted. Its situation as a high-risk country (political risk, given the prevailing instability, and economic risk, given its dependence on its energy resources alone) meant that it was only entitled to short-term loans at higher rates, accentuating its financial dependence. At the same time, imports were on the rise due to demographic pressure: they represented 8.5 billion dollars, including 2.5 billion for food. And let's not forget the evil that plagues all totalitarian regimes: corruption. In fact, kickbacks accounted for around 15% of total transactions. They were - and still are - shared between all the protagonists. Half of these commissions are deducted by foreign firms for various reasons, such as the additional cost of international credit, or country risk, while the other half is divided equally between commissions paid to managers of exporting firms and commissions paid into foreign accounts to our officials. In Algeria, specifications are drawn up according to the chosen supplier: a transaction with China costs less than one with Italy, Spain or France. The various phases of the transaction are meticulously monitored under the patronage of one of the regime's high-ranking dignitaries, each with his or her own sphere of action. The money is transferred to a foreign account under the name of a close relative or trusted businessman.

In Algeria, for example, the portfolio of the Minister of the Interior is responsible for land and market allocation, the portfolio of the Minister of Finance for credit and customs facilities, and the portfolio of the Minister of Justice for impunity in the event of legal problems.

These ministerial posts were only granted after approval by the Generals. The case of Mahi Bahi, former Minister of Justice, who was dismissed on November 14, 1992 for having attacked magistrates and examining magistrates suspected of corruption, without the approval of the decision-makers, is one of the most significant examples from the early 1990s.

It was against this backdrop of serious, multi-structural crisis that Belaïd Abdeslam formed his government on July 19, 1992. Eleven days after its formation, he took on the post of Finance Minister in addition to that of head of government. On August 10, 1992, he advocated a wartime economy, refused to devalue the dinar and decided to reduce imports, but the crisis only got worse. Belaïd Abdeslam was soon confronted with the reality of his appointment: he was merely a pawn on the chessboard. The military decision-makers had no intention of giving him the green light he needed to implement his program, which, by the way, was utopian. Worse still, according to Belaïd Abdeslam's testimony, General Nezzar rejected his strategy of changing banknotes to combat tax evasion. And during the Nezzar-Souaïdia trial, Benderra, the former president of Crédit Populaire, explained very clearly how the military had deliberately chosen immobility, leading to certain bankruptcy in 1994.

Just a few days after Mohamed Boudiaf's funeral, and in the midst of national mourning, Mohamed Lamari, Khalifa Rahim, Derradji, Djennouhat and Djouadi were promoted to the rank of major general.

On July 7, 1992, the first large-scale sweep was launched against the strongholds of Abdelkader Chebouti's troops in Lakhdaria, Aïn Defla and Constantine. A large number of Chebouti members were killed or arrested, and all these strongholds were taken over by the troops of Mansouri Miliani's group, which later became the GIA. Never in the history of modern guerrilla warfare has an armed group worked against its own interests, threatening its very existence, as the GIA did. At the Baba Hassen meeting, Moh Leveilly, emir of the Groupe du Centre for several days thanks to Mansouri Meliani, refused to join the other warlords. After the meeting, he was shot dead by security forces on his way home. He was succeeded by Abdelhak Layada, who accused Abdelkader Chebouti and Saïd Mekhloufi of being behind his death and of being traitors in the service of the military. But Abdelhak Layada's work was perplexing to many specialists. Despite his rather limited intellectual capacities, in just four months he succeeded in creating, establishing and federating armed groups throughout the country; he provided the material resources (communications, weapons, money) and found the men. Nicknamed "le tôlier" by the Algerian press in reference to his pre-war profession, Abdelhak Layada divided Algeria into war zones. Each region is divided into zones, and each zone is divided according to the number of *katibats* ("companies"), which in turn are divided according to the number of *sarayats* ("cells"). So when Layada proclaimed himself leader of the armed Islamic groups in January 1993, he knew that he controlled virtually all the armed groups throughout the country. Was he a military genius or simply a sheet metal worker in the service of the DRS?

After his arrest in Morocco on June 10, 1993, and extradition to Algeria two months later, he was incarcerated in Serkadji prison, although the security services were unable to dismantle at least the group's structure.

Mourad Sid Ahmed, known as "Djaafer El Afghani", succeeded him as national emir of the GIA. Shortly afterwards, he executed a member of his own council, one of former Emir Abdelhak Layada's right-hand men, accusing him of being an undercover secret service agent. This agent, nicknamed "Rafik", was not only the former emir's right-hand man, but also emir of the "Company of Death" (*"Katibat El Mout"*). His right-hand man was Djamel Zitouni. At the time, this *katibat* had already carried out a number of attacks against foreigners and intellectuals, but it was above all involved in the kidnapping of the three agents from the French consulate in Algiers.

On September 26, 1992, General Lamari was appointed head of the Centre de Conduite et de Coordination des Actions de Lutte Anti-Subversive[83] (CCCALAS), which brings together the army's special forces units in charge of fighting terrorism. Lamari found himself at the head of an elite troop of ten thousand men, becoming the strongest man in the system.

On September 30, 1992, Legislative Decree No. 93-03 on the fight against subversion and terrorism, known as the "anti-terrorism law", was promulgated and came into force the following day. On October 31, 1992, Algiers recorded its first bomb attack, at the Riad-El-Feth shopping mall, killing four people. A month later, on November 30, a curfew was decreed in the center of the country. Town halls and associations linked to the FIS were dissolved. This curfew led to appalling fear in the capital. Night-time sweeps following daytime attacks became increasingly frequent. This led to

---

83. *Ibid*, p. 657.

the emergence of "death squads" known as "Squadron 192" (in reference to January 1st, the year of the coup d'état), which specialized in disappearances and extrajudicial executions. The first victims of this repressive system were the military themselves, and all those who did not obey the official eradicatory line. Indeed, between December 17 and 30, 1992, the Bechar court sentenced 92 soldiers for belonging to the FIS. On the same day, Roger Guyon, a French convert to Islam, was sentenced to death by the Algiers court for membership of a terrorist group. He will be handed over to the French authorities as a gesture of goodwill.

A few weeks later, on February 13, 1993, France granted five billion francs in trade credits to Algeria[84], and provided two billion dollars in aid for the whole of 1993. Roland Dumas, followed shortly afterwards by Finance Minister Michel Sapin on February 13, 1993, paid a visit to Algiers on January 8 and 9, 1993, where he declared that France would support Algeria in its difficulties. The year 1993 marked a decisive turning point in Algeria's political and economic life. Following the HCS's renewal of the HCE for a further year, the ruling Generals used every trick in the book to convince the West of the wisdom of halting the electoral process, in order to protect the Algerian people - and indeed the West - from the fundamentalist organ.

General Nezzar had understood, albeit a little later than General Belkheir, that it was necessary to remain in the

---

84. *Ibid*, p. 724.

shadows, and above all to choose a controllable foal to replace him. On February 13, 1993, General Guenaizia, Nezzar's childhood and school friend, was replaced on the General Staff by General Mohamed Lamari, who was assigned to the Algerian Embassy in Switzerland to keep a close eye on his accumulated fortunes. But this golden retirement was above all a means of clearing the way for Lamari. Guenaizia had shown a certain reluctance when Chadli Bendjeddid was deposed. Nezzar played the security card, especially with the appointment of Zeroual.

A pseudo car-bomb attack was carried out against General Nezzar, without injuring him. Five months later, he appointed Liamine Zeroual in his place, despite the conflict between them in 1988, but naturally imposed his own advisors on the new Minister of Defense. A few days earlier, on July 5, 1993, Larbi Belkheir's protégé, Smaïn Lamari, had been promoted to the rank of general[85]. Once the balance of power between the two strongmen had been secured, it was time to find a civilian personality endowed with cynicism and opportunism, who would serve as a showcase by assuming political and economic responsibility for the country. The choice was simple: Reda Malek, above all because a few days earlier, during a visit to France from June 16 to 18, 1993, he had been endorsed by foreign financial backers. On August 21, 1993, he was appointed Prime Minister, replacing Belaïd Abdeslam who had failed

---

85. *Annuaire de l'Afrique du Nord (1993)*, p. 422.

to convince the Paris Club during his visit to the French capital from February 18 to 20, 1993. On the day Reda Malek was appointed Prime Minister, the former head of Military Security, Kasdi Merbah, was assassinated in Bordj-El-Bahri, along with his brother, his son and his Praetorian Guard. The attack was claimed by the GIA, and condemned by the entire political class, including the various tendencies of the FIS. The day before his death, Kasdi Merbah was on a trip to Switzerland, and had managed to reach an agreement with the Islamist leaders in exile to start a dialogue. According to *Maghreb Confidentiel* of June 16, 1994, Kasdi Merbah was negotiating with the Islamists for Zeroual. He was part of the anti-Nezzar clan, loyal to Boumediene's legacy. But the "death squads" had other ideas, as Kasdi Merbah represented not only a danger to their political and economic project, but also to their very future. Wasn't one of the causes of Mohamed Boudiaf's death his closeness to Kasdi Merbah? The most vigilant man in Algeria was bound to be brought down by professionals who knew perfectly well his instincts and mannerisms. Before his death, to a journalist who asked him for his assessment of democracy, he replied: "Let's stop improvising. We made predictions, as we did with Chadli's resignation, and they proved to be right. We also told the late Mohamed Boudiaf that, because of some of his positions on dialogue in particular, there could be problems before the end of the semester. We didn't expect it to end in assassination. The country is going through a serious crisis, and in our opinion, there isn't a group of people capable of resolving it alone. We need to be driven by the national interest, with the aim of building a democracy on sound foundations. To do this, we need to organize a dialogue, and decide all together on a political program concerning the resumption of the democratic process, the presidential elections, the role of the parties, their access to the media, and check that the parties are committed to respecting a certain number of principles as we have done within the Group of Seven."

Add to this the long list of political assassinations that were beginning to take hold: those of Sanhadji, Liabes, Flici, Djaout, Boucebci, Boukhobza...

On November 26, 1993, Bouslimani, Nahnah's dauphin, was kidnapped by a mysterious organization called the Organization of Free Algerian Youth (OJAL) and the GIA (according to Abdelkader Tigha's testimony, the OJAL is a pseudo-organization created by the DRS in November 1993 to capture the imagination of civilians). Two months later, he was found murdered near Birtouta. On December 10, 1993, General Touati approached six founding members of the FIS to participate in a possible dialogue. In effect, the decision-makers proposed dialogue, in the knowledge that within the FIS, the radical faction controlled by the security services would set the bar very high, thus providing the authorities with an alibi for breaking off dialogue at a later date, and shifting from the role of torturer to that of victim. Among the FIS's first demands for a return to normal life were those of Rabah Kebir: the release of political detainees, the repeal of laws and regulations adopted after the electoral process was halted, the choice of a neutral country for the establishment of a dialogue, the creation of a commission of inquiry... The authorities categorically refused, and once again brought in their best FIS asset, Hachemi Sahnouni, to add fuel to the fire: he declared that a new transition would only aggravate the crisis. The government, adept at manipulation, false dialogue and diversionary tactics, tried to convince the other parties to take part in a national conference whose sole purpose was to endorse the candidate chosen by the military to lead the state. But the first choice, Abdelaziz Bouteflika, withdrew, considering that he did not have all the necessary guarantees to accomplish his mission. He eventually accepted to be appointed President of the Republic a few years later. The Generals were forced to use another joker: retired General Liamine Zeroual. After the usual demonstrations of support for a totalitarian country, organized by the security services, the HCS approved this choice. Zeroual, without warning anyone, took the initiative of establishing contacts with the imprisoned FIS leaders, infuriating the military.

Faced with the fear that the protégé chosen by Nezzar and his cohorts, galvanized by his dual role as Head of State and Minister of Defense, might take flight and turn against his mentors, the army's top brass met in total secrecy on March 17, 18 and 19. They decided to grant a delegation of signatures to General Major Mohamed Lamari, Chief of the Army Staff. Reda Malek was dismissed and replaced by Mokdad Sifi on April 13, 1994. Before his departure, the decision-makers made him endorse the agreements reached with the IMF: for example, he signed the 40% devaluation of the dinar, which led to a sharp rise in the price of basic necessities. On May 24, 1994, the provisions of corporate autonomy prohibiting the introduction of domestic or foreign private capital were abolished.

In May 1994, a major reshuffle took place in the upper echelons of the army. According to *Intelligence Online* (July 26, 1994), two groups of generals clashed: Zeroual's clan on the one hand, and Nezzar's on the other.

Salah Gaïd replaced Rahim Khalifa at the CFT (Corps des Forces Terrestres), Mohamed Benslimane replaced Mokhtar Boutamine at the head of the air force, while Gheziel, Ghodbane and Achour were retained at the head of their corps. As for the military regions, they all underwent changes, the most important of which was the assignment of the DCSA boss to head the 4th region. Two years later, according to General Nezzar's version, he was killed in a car accident on a straight, deserted road, while the MAOL (Mouvement Algérien des Officiers Libres) accused Smaïn Lamari's "death squads" of executing him with an explosive charge placed under his car. Following this affair, Zeroual appointed a commission of inquiry, the results of which will not be known to anyone. According to MAOL, the dispute between Smaïn Lamari and Saïdi Fodhil goes back to the so-called JOBE affair, which almost provoked a diplomatic incident between Algeria and Switzerland: Smaïn Lamari, through the intermediary of the head of the Bureau des Services de Sécurité (BSS) in Geneva, had recruited on his own account an agent of the Swiss services in charge of surveillance of Algerian Islamists, without the approval of Saïdi Fodhil, on whom he depended organically. As for the latter, the press reported in June 1995 that he had been appointed head of the national gendarmerie, in place of General Gheziel, but he never joined this post. It should be remembered that Gheziel was one of the four generals who forced their way into Chadli's office to depose him.

On June 18, Fathallah[86], president of the government-affiliated Human Rights League, was assassinated. After his death, tongues were wagging. The assassination was linked to the Boudiaf affair: Fathallah was a member of the commission of inquiry[87]. He had expressed his reluctance to sign the final report, a gesture that the decision-makers could not let pass so as not to set a precedent, and above all to silence a person who had learned a great deal about the affair. On July 15, the GIA claimed responsibility for the kidnapping of two Arab ambassadors, from Yemen and the Sultanate of Oman. After a wave of protests, international outrage and total condemnation of this act, they were released.

On August 27, Algeria closed its borders with Morocco after the Moroccan authorities imposed an entry visa on Algerian nationals. A few days later, Morocco accused the

---

86. Mohamed Samraoui, *op. cit.* p. 262.
87. Youcef Zirem, *op. cit.* p. 22.

Algerian state of being behind the attacks in Marrakech and Fez. On September 25, one day before the death of GIA emir Cherif Gousmi, Kabyle singer Lounès Matoub was kidnapped by an armed group. He was released unharmed on October 10, following the unprecedented mobilization of the whole of Kabylia.

On October 31, 1994, Mohamed Lamari was promoted to the rank of Lieutenant General. After the meeting, Liamine Zeroual realized that he could not be a legitimate president without being elected. Faced with a lack of confidence on the part of his own friends, he played the card of former service bosses. He called on the former Minister of Defense, General Betchine, who became his advisor. Aided by this dinosaur of the seraglio, on October 31, 1994, Liamine Zeroual announced the organization of a presidential election that would provide him with the legitimacy he lacked. A year later, he was elected President of the Republic. Faced with pressure from military deci-sion-makers, however, he backed down on the FIS issue. He left it to the security services to use their best trump cards among the armed groups, in order to undermine the credibility of the Islamist insurrection in the eyes of a population battered by the war.

Djamel Zitouni was chosen from among many others to succeed Cherif Gousmi, who was shot dead in September 1994 near Saoula while carrying a letter from Ali Benhadj urging him to continue the jihad. Djamel Zitouni's appointment as GIA national emir in October

1994 remains controversial. According to some sources, he was behind the assassination of Cherif Gousmi, who was sold to the security forces when he was due to meet a man known as "Napoli", head of the central group. Under Djamel Zitouni, the GIA excelled in barbarity, but above all did the job hoped for by a fringe group of generals, and fulfilled one of the wishes of Reda Malek, who had declared some time earlier "that fear [should] change sides". He executed the entire FIS leadership underground, and ruthlessly punished all FIS supporters, massacring and uprooting entire villages. According to some analysts, Djamel Zitouni was an agent of the DRS, while others, such as Abdelkader Tigha[88], believe that "Djamel Zitouni was used indirectly, via Emir Merdj Abdelkrim, a former volunteer imam from the town of Boufarik (Blida), recruited by the DRS in Blida".

We also need to involve the international community, and France in particular, in this logic of war against the Islamist organ, by exporting this terror to foreign soil. The hijacking of the Air France Airbus at Algiers airport on December 24, 1994, the Paris bombings in the summer of 1995 and the massacre of the monks of Tibhirine in 1996 provided the support the generals in Algiers had been hoping for, enabling them to save their war booty: oil.

On November 1st, Independence Day, the GIA's new emir carried out a cowardly and despicable attack on young

---

88. www.algeria-watch.de

scouts at the cemetery in the town of Mostaganem, where they had come to pay their respects. It moved the entire Algerian people.

After the debt rescheduling agreement signed with the Paris Club on June 1st, another agreement was reached with the United States on December 15. But these agreements were conditional on the application of the shock therapy dictated by the IMF following Algeria's financial collapse. The IMF imposed a halt to subsidies to public enterprises, the closure of non-viable companies, with the consequent mass lay-offs of 400,000 workers, and the devaluation of the dinar. At the same time, the Generals turned to business thanks to a portion of the loans granted by the IMF following the rescheduling agreement. This also enabled them to recycle dirty money from corruption and procurement commissions into import-import companies, real estate, insurance companies and banks. At the end of 1994, a study carried out by experts from a private Swiss bank showed that the assets of Algerians abroad had reached thirty-four billion dollars, including seventeen billion in France[89].

Where did this money come from and who owned it? It's by answering these questions that we may be able to understand this second war imposed on the Algerian people, a people reduced to misery, half of whom live below the poverty line on less than a dollar a day, while the

---

89. Ali Yahia Abdenour, *op. cit.* p. 142.

privileged few belonging to the ruling caste display their wads of cash in Europe's biggest squares.

The hijacking of the Air France Airbus

On December 24, 1994, an Airbus belonging to the French airline Air France was hijacked by a four-man GIA commando unit at Algiers airport, despite the draconian measures taken since the attack of August 1992. Three hostages were executed during the hijacking: an Algerian policeman, a Vietnamese diplomat and a French cook working at the French embassy in Algiers. Two days later, the Groupe d'Intervention de la Gendarmerie Nationale (GIGN) stormed the hijacked plane at Marseille's Marignane airport. The four terrorists were killed and all the passengers freed, averting a crash over Paris.

When I left the Blida military prison in November 1995, the name of a policeman belonging to the Bab Ezzouar anti-terrorist squad was mentioned to me several times in the neighborhood where I lived, bearing witness to the terrorist horde's relentless pursuit of blameless members of the police force. Toufik was killed just a few days after the Airbus hijacking affair, in an ambush in Bab Ezzouar, not far from the police station, where two anti-terrorist police cars were destroyed by terrorist fire. Of the eight occupants, only one miraculously escaped death.

Toufik came from a modest family living in the Eucalyptus district. He had chosen to join the police force, while his brother had taken up arms against the government and joined the Islamist maquis. Toufik and his colleagues were the first to arrive at Algiers airport on the day the plane was hijacked. They were the ones who set up the security perimeter: Algiers airport is located in Dar El Baïda, the former Maison Blanche, part of the Bab Ezzouar sub-prefecture. And Toufik was a member of the Mobile Brigade of the Judicial Police (BMPJ) of this sub-prefecture. The first preliminary investigation was carried out by this BMPJ. These officers noted that no person - civilian, police officer or member of another security corps, whatever their rank - could arrive at the tarmac, not on foot, not by bus, not even in a police car, without an authorization granted by the officer in charge of security, whose code and password could only be known on the day of duty by him and the personnel placed under his authority.

The hostage-takers' police cards and passes were not forged. The police officers were removed from the security perimeter to make way only for DRS elements, provoking their anger. The few journalists who had access to the file revealed a number of anomalies that arouse suspicion: the last-minute defection of the real instigator of the affair, Yahia Rihane[90] aka "Kronfel", originally from Birkhadem (the same district where Emir Zitouni was shot dead in March 1997); the confidences made to Catherine Beugnet[91], the cook's

90. Based on Omar Chikhi's account of the composition of the commando "passed under silence", France 3, May 2002.
91. Testimony of Yannick Beugnet's wife on M6 and in *Sud-Ouest* on January 4, 2005.

The False Democratization Process and the Second Algerian War (1989-2007)

wife, by a third party working at Air France to prevent her husband from taking the plane: "He must leave tomorrow absolutely, if necessary I'll make him sit in the cockpit."

In his testimony, Samraoui, the former number two in Algerian counter-espionage at the time, cites the death, on December 24, of an airport commissioner who had advised several passengers against taking the flight, as well as the rumor circulating in Islamist circles that the plane was to carry a foreign military delegation, the failure to investigate the case and bring it to trial, and the fact that the hijacking occurred just after the first meeting of the political opposition in Rome, which later led to the famous Rome contract.

The Rome contract: refusal of a consensual alternative

Algeria plunged into violence. The interruption of the electoral process in December 1991, the arrest of FIS leaders and cadres, the introduction of a state of emergency and the closure of the political field, coupled with a disastrous economic situation, plunged Algeria into the abyss. To break out of the violent duality between armed Islamist groups and the security forces, and to give a voice back to the people, the Algerian political class (almost all of them, apart from a few microscopic parties) met in Rome under the aegis of San Egidio. They couldn't meet in Algiers, where the authorities had initiated nothing but bogus dialogues as a smokescreen for unilateral decisions and the policy of fait accompli. The aim was to find ways of putting an end to the violence in Algeria, which, according to some NGOs, had already claimed over fifty thousand lives and left thousands missing. A first meeting took place on November 21, 1994, bringing together sixteen personalities: leaders of political parties, human rights activists and religious figures. Among those present were: Abdelhamid Mehri, General Secretary of the FLN, Hocine Ait Ahmed, President of the FFS, Ahmed Ben Bella, President of the MDA and former President of the Republic, Mahfoudh Nahnah, President of Hamas, Abdellah Djaballah, President of Nahda[92], Ali Yahia Abdenour, president of the Ligue de Défense des Droits de l'Homme, Louisa Hanoune, spokeswoman for the Parti des Travailleurs, Noureddine Boukrouh, president of the Parti du Renouveau Algérien (later a minister in Ouyahia's government), Ahmed Benmohamed (JMC), and the FIS represented by Anouar Haddam.

Mahfoudh Nahnah and Noureddine Boukrouh withdrew from the second meeting, only to lend their support a few months later to the election of Liamine Zeroual as President of the Republic. On January 13, 1995, after several days of negotiations, the participants drew up a platform for resolving the Algerian crisis, stressing the urgent need for a comprehensive, political and equitable solution. The platform stressed "respect for human rights, the rejection of all forms of violence to gain

---

92. After the split in 1997, he created the Mouvement National du Renouveau (National Renewal Movement), of which he became president; the MNR is currently considered the second most powerful political force in Algeria.

or maintain power, and respect for political alternation through universal suffrage"; it enshrined a multi-party system, the separation of legislative, judicial and executive powers, and freedom and respect for religious beliefs; it reaffirmed the constituent elements of the Algerian personality (Islam, Arabness, Amazighness), the rejection of any dictatorship whatever its form; it guaranteed fundamental individual and collective freedoms, respect for "popular legitimacy", and also called on the army "not to become involved in political affairs and to return to its role of safeguarding the unity and indivisibility of the territory". These objectives were to be preceded by "measures of détente with an appeal to FIS leaders to cease violence, and the release of political detainees, the closure of concentration camps and the lifting of the state of emergency by the military authorities". But the authorities rejected this consensual alternative put forward by the entire opposition, which proposed a political solution to the crisis. It called the participants agents in the pay of foreign forces, and accused the San Egidio community of interference in Algeria's internal affairs.

The true nature of power was revealed: that of a totalitarian power that had no desire whatsoever to resolve the crisis peacefully, clinging to its attributes, ignoring all avenues open to citizens, and obsessed by the idea of being forced to give decision-making and management power to unsponsored Algerian citizens.

The Serkadji prison massacre

The Serkadji prison massacre took place at a time when the Algerian people were plunged into terror, and resulted in the deaths of tens of thousands of citizens. To understand the reasons behind this massacre, we need to recall the succession of spectacular escapes achieved by Islamists largely infiltrated by the DRS within Algerian prisons. Some of these escapes can only be explained by the fact that they were deliberate, as the presence of extremely dangerous terrorists in these prisons had led to the introduction of draconian security measures.

The first large-scale escape was from Tazoult, where 1,200 prisoners, most of them convicted of terrorist acts, managed to escape. This escape, which involved a symbol of high security, provoked the resignation of the Prefect of Batna. The Lambèse prison is considered a fortress where escape is impossible. It has its own security system, backed up by an emergency response program that provides for intervention within fifteen minutes. This spectacular escape therefore remains a mystery. Questions remain unanswered to this day: how could an escape on such a scale have escaped the notice of the intelligence services, when they were able to dismantle even the smallest terrorist support networks? Why was the intervention of the security forces delayed? Why, a few days earlier, had almost all the figures of bloodthirsty terrorism been transferred to this prison? Why had Madani Mezrag, within the Islamic Salvation Army, accepted only the most reliable men from among the fugitives, who already belonged to his group?

Some of these questions are answered by the advent of Djamel Zitouni as head of the GIA, and by the drift of this group. Hadn't Djamel Zitouni adopted a number of his members as advisors? He was to take over the leadership of the GIA and needed support to establish his authority, and there was no better way to achieve this infiltration into the GIA than by faking an escape. Incidentally, there were no FIS leaders in the prison. Most of them were either in Berrouaghia prison or in Serkadji.

The second event was the Berrouaghia prison massacre, perpetrated in the autumn of 1994, following an escape attempt. Mustapha, a local man who had served five years in this prison for membership of a terrorist group, explained to me on his release that, a few days before that fateful day, which according to him cost the lives of over a hundred prisoners, the rumor of the escape had spread so widely in the prison yard that he had had difficulty reaching the infirmary for treatment. An academic by training, Mustapha doubted the sincerity of the group behind the escape; its members, who had arrived at the prison only a few months earlier, said they had managed to coax a guard into contact with their brothers on the outside, who were supposed to be waiting for them outside the prison to help them join the Islamist maquis. On the day in question, all the prisoners who had just passed through the prison gates were shot dead by a waiting elite brigade. The remaining prisoners, who were not caught in the ambush, were surrounded inside the prison and shot.

Mustapha explained to me that the hardest thing was to stay alive after such a tragedy, with the remorse of not having been able to avoid it. During my stay at Serkadji prison between 1999 and 2000, long-term prisoners described to me the scenario of the tragedy: atrocious acts committed with knives by a small number of mutineers on other prisoners and prison guards; summary executions; mutilations carried out by elements of the special services on prisoners who had absolutely nothing to do with the mutiny. And the prisoners were executed in two ways: some individually in their cells, others as a group in the exercise yard.

Mustapha told me: "Everything happened so fast. When it happened, time had no meaning. I don't remember how many days it lasted. Two or three days[93]." He remembers that one of the guards inside the first block, known as Rtila ("spider"), narrowly managed to get through the main door into the blocks, and set off the alarm. Serkadji prison is divided into two blocks: the old Turkish prison, and the new French prison. Islamist prisoners occupy the old block, while ordinary prisoners occupy the new one.

The prison is laid out as follows: the entrance to the blocks is on the same side as that for ordinary prisoners. This section also contains the library, kitchen, showers, hairdressing salon, bakery, waiting room, central infirmary and head

---

93. February 20-22, 1995.

warden's office. The old Turkish prison is separated from the new one by gates on all three floors. It includes the infirmary, the high-security rooms where death row inmates are held, and the exercise yards. Behind the central door giving access to the blocks are the clerk's office and the lawyers' room, as well as the visiting room. On the other side of the central entrance, towards the blocks, are the warden's office and dormitory, and behind the prison watchtowers, the gendarmerie high command barracks.

By the time the guard raised the alarm, some of his colleagues had already been stabbed to death by the dozen or so mutineers. Some of them had burst into the blocks of common prisoners, looking for a solution, but the prison was already surrounded. "I only saw one mutineer with a gun (according to the authorities, there were four). He was stationed at the traffic circle on the second floor, facing the entrance gate. Then they headed for the room where the police officers were being held. They took them out one by one. After sorting them out, they took them down to the convicts' yard and slit their throats in turn. Then all of a sudden everything stopped, no more comings and goings, a deathly silence. The special forces then intervened, the famous 'ninjas', who entered through the terrace windows, using toxic gas. Some of the inmates fainted, asphyxiated. They quickly occupied the part of the prison reserved for common law prisoners, then fired heavily, while ordering the inmates to return to their cells. The inmates ran in all directions, taking refuge wherever they could. During the assault, some common law prisoners were taken to the block of Islamist prisoners. They were considered mutineers and executed. The hard core took refuge in the basement of 21. A loud explosion was heard. Most of the Islamist convicts were executed. Some of those not on trial were spared, as were a few inmates who had guards on their payroll (at Serkadji, a guard is paid between one thousand and one thousand five hundred dinars for the transmission of a letter, and a cell phone call costs ten thousand dinars). Others were spared by order."

After a moment's absence, Mustapha stared at me and said: "The hardest part was afterwards, with the imposed diet. Everything was forbidden, even the visiting room." He looked up at the walls of the blocks facing the courtyard and continued, "See that black smoke on the windows? It dates back to the events. Even with several coats of paint since then, it just won't go away." Then he shut up and stood up.

The police investigation revealed the names of the instigators, including the leader of the mutineers, a certain Belkacem, an Islamist prisoner condemned to death, who was allegedly approached by a guard to organize the escape. The guard was said to have family members in the armed groups. Belkacem was a new defector. His incarceration in this prison was not even a year old. Among their contacts on the outside was a certain Omar Abdelhafid, a teenager from the cité douanière district of El-Harrach, on the outskirts of Algiers. All his neighbors were astonished to read his name on the list quoted by the press, because at the time of the events, he had already been arrested (he is now one of the missing persons of the last decade).

So the question is simple. Why this laissez-faire attitude, if there was such a thing? And why, just a few days earlier, had certain Islamist figures been transferred to Serkadji prison? Didn't the Serkadji and Berrouaghia cases mark the beginning of the physical elimination of certain FIS figures, which Zitouni himself completed six months later? In a country governed by the rule of law, when a citizen makes a mistake, it's the justice system that takes charge and applies the law. But what does the law have in store when it's the state that flouts its own laws within the sanctuary of justice?

The story of this young teenager, who was passed off as the instigator of this pseudo-escape which led to the death of over a hundred prisoners (according to the official version), even though he had been arrested a few days earlier, should certainly be clarified one day.

Horror scenes from Algiers to Paris

On January 30, 1995, a car-bomb attack was carried out on the central police station in Algiers, killing some 40 people and injuring a hundred more. Most of those killed were ordinary citizens on the busy Boulevard Amirouche. Djamel Zitouni, the GIA's new emir, had just signed the beginning of a remote-controlled criminal battle.

On July 11, 1995, terrorism crossed the Mediterranean to strike France. Sahraoui Abdelbaki, a founding member of the FIS who had delivered the preaching proclaiming the party's birth, was coldly executed by a gunman inside the prayer hall of the Myrha mosque in Paris's 18th arrondissement, just after the *el asr* prayer. A young man, who was inside the mosque at the time, was also killed for trying to catch the killer. Once the prayer was over, the imam was approached by someone who wanted to talk to him face-to-face. As the mosque emptied, the assassin drew his gun and fired. The imam collapsed. Nordine, a young member of the Fraternité Algérienne en France (FAF) was still in the mosque; seeing the scene, he grabbed the assassin and tackled him to the ground. Unfortunately, none of the worshippers still outside the mosque door came to his aid. The second killer, who was standing guard at the door, shot him in the back. The two killers, joined by a third accomplice outside, hurried up Rue Myrha, but without concern, even though one of them was covered in blood. At the end of rue Laghouat, they held up a woman, took her car and abandoned it a little further down rue du Nord. They then took another car, which they dared to park at the foot of the building where they had taken up residence. Was this first attack by the GIA on one of the most closely watched people on French soil linked to the imam's knowledge of a probable attack being prepared in Paris? Was he preparing to denounce the criminals when the time was right?

On July 25, 1995, a gas cylinder exploded in an RER train at Saint-Michel station in Paris, killing eight people and injuring eighty-three others. This act of terrorism was followed by five others and two other attempts that narrowly failed: on August 17, a gas cylinder exploded in the 8th arrondissement of Paris, injuring seventeen people; on August 26, an attempted attack on the Lyon-Paris TGV line; on September 3, a bomb exploded on boulevard Richard-Lenoir, injuring four people; on September 4, a car exploded in front of a Jewish school, injuring fourteen people; on October 6, a bomb exploded at the Maison-Blanche metro station in Paris, injuring thirteen people; on October 17, a bomb exploded on the RER C, injuring twenty-nine people. The wave of terrorist attacks in France left eight people dead and one hundred and ninety-eight injured. On September 29, 1995, Khaled Kelkal was shot dead by French security forces, taking with him some of the secrets behind the attacks. As for his emir, Ali Touchent aka "Tarek", he managed to slip through the net. His death was announced in a communiqué issued by the Algerian security services in May 1997. But who could verify the veracity of this announcement? According to the testimony of his brother[94], the man sent by the DRS version of the GIA emir was a double agent also working for the Direction de la Sûreté du Territoire (DST). Spotted in Belgium and France between 1993 and 1995, Ali Touchent escaped at least three police raids. He apparently had the flair of a James Bond, but he didn't save his family and accomplices. And yet, the man who always preferred to travel by container between

---

94. *Libération*, October 6, 2002.

the port of Algiers and the port of Marseille was not hiding in Algeria at all. He even lived in a luxurious apartment in a government housing estate near Châteauneuf (close to the famous barracks whose grounds are said by Algerian rumors to be overflowing with the bodies of the disappeared). For a wanted emir, he lived quietly until the famous GIA trial in November 1997, when he was directly implicated. Several defendants pointed to him as an Algerian security service agent who had infiltrated the GIA: "For me, Tarek is a guy from the Algerian Military Security who used us[95]", as one witness explained.

A few months later, in February 1998, the Algerian authorities announced that he had died almost ten months earlier. Why was this? Was it because the Algeria of the Generals could no longer cover up for a person of no importance, once he had fulfilled his role?

While all the men suspected of the above-mentioned attacks were supposed to have been arrested, another attack contradicted this thesis. On December 3, 1996, a bomb blamed on the GIA exploded at the Port-Royal RER station in Paris, killing four people and injuring 170. On December 12, 1996, the newspaper *Le Monde* revealed that, in a memo sent to the Élysée and Matignon departments fourteen days before the attack, the French espionage service considered the resumption of Islamist terrorist operations likely. In all these matters, I believe that the

---

95. *Ibid.*

The False Democratization Process and the Second Algerian War (1989-2007)

interests of justice must take precedence over the interests of business. Ali Touchent, Tarek or the ghost who travels in containers between Algiers and Marseille, remain the same criminal, but it's only a drop in an ocean of blood. In October 2002, Boualem Ben Saïd, "the mastermind of the Paris attacks" according to the press, was sentenced to life imprisonment for only three attacks, including the Saint-Michel attack for complicity. Who, then, is behind the others? According to *Maghreb Confidentiel* of April 18, 1996, a meeting between French services and Algerian generals took place in February in Nice. On the French side, there were General Rondot and Jean-Charles Marchiani; and on the Algerian side, General Touati and General Nezzar. According to the same source, this was a regular meeting between the two services.

Zeroual's election in November 1995

To legitimize Zeroual's election, the security services, through the GIA, stepped up the violence against citizens, increasing fear tenfold by means of a propaganda system using subservient newspapers and heavyweight media. After the advent of Liamine Zeroual as head of state, and Mohamed Lamari as army chief, Algeria embarked on a new war strategy: at all costs, it was necessary to protect the useful[96] Algeria from any armed conflict.

---

96. In other words, the places in Algeria that generate profits for the Generals (the Sahara, the ports, certain districts...).

In April 1995, a decree issued by the Minister of the Interior, effective May [1,] announced the creation of exclusion zones in the South. Access was strictly regulated and limited to oil company personnel working in the area. Site security was ensured by highly-equipped military units. Foreign companies had their own security strategies for recruiting agents.

It was also necessary to break up the Islamist rebellion by fuelling ideological division, and to exacerbate tensions between the various emirs for control of the maquis, a task which would be taken on by infiltrators. Thus, at the meeting of May 13, 1994, we witnessed a regrouping of the different sensibilities of Algerian armed Islamism under the umbrella of the GIA. The Islamists close to the Nahda doctrinaire line refused to join this coalition and created the Armée Islamique du Salut (Islamic Salvation Army) in July 1994. But this union did not last. A merciless war broke out a few weeks later between the various factions for control of the maquis. Initially limited to a conflict between the AIS and the GIA, this war spread over the months to other armed groups, including the MEI, which withdrew from the GIA coalition in August 1994. This fratricidal struggle culminated in the annihilation by GIA leader Djamel Zitouni of the FIS cadres who had chosen to take up arms. Over one hundred and forty FIS cadres were executed between July 1995 and February 1996, leading to the break-up of the GIA and a dozen other armed groups.

The military also used all available means to defeat Islamist groups that were getting out of hand. A large-scale operation was carried out between March 19 and 22, 1995 in Aïn Defla, in western Algeria, during which the GIA lost over three hundred fighters, including famous emirs. At the same time, the press was put under pressure to take a clear and definitive stand in favor of the military. The recalcitrant were dismissed. In the course of that year, the press lost a number of prestigious titles, either by court order or through economic collapse, following the disappearance of the advertising windfall under state control. The number of journalists murdered increased, some by armed Islamist groups, others still unsolved. Were they the work of Islamist groups manipulated by the services or by them directly? By wielding hatred, the press found itself, in spite of itself, the first shield against an invisible enemy whose name it only knew: GIA.

At the same time, we had to act quickly to respond to the IMF's injunctions and restore our tarnished image. The most vulnerable will suffer the consequences. But the decision-makers, faithful to their tradition of showering the Algerian people with promises, will take advantage of this windfall to arm themselves, buy their supporters, pay the militiamen, and retrain their offspring in the lucrative import-import trade. All the tragedies of the Algerian people have been exploited to good effect: for example, the "Air Algérie" affair, with the suspension of the Algiers-Paris route, has enabled the scavengers of the system to monopolize passenger transport from Lyon or Charleroi to Paris, and they have done everything in their power to ensure that this route is no longer served.

Presidential elections were held on November 16, 1995. The GIA threatened reprisals against citizens who voted, while militiamen armed by the authorities threatened them if they did not. These elections, under the protection of bayonets, were rigged, as were all the others, of course. Liamine Zeroual was elected President of the Republic with 61.34% of the votes cast, well ahead of stooges Mahfoudh Nahnah (25.39%), Saïd Saadi (9.29%) and Noureddine Boukrouh (3.98%). On December 30, 1995, Ahmed Ouyahia, Zeroual's chief of staff, was appointed head of government to implement the austerity program imposed by the IMF. Hundreds of thousands of workers found themselves unemployed, dozens of factories closed. Purchasing power collapsed, prices soared: the days of elections and promises were over.

The missing

How many people are missing? That's the question the authorities don't want to answer. The number of people who have disappeared over the last decade varies between ten and twenty thousand, according to estimates by various NGOs and human rights activists. Most of these were carried out by the security services. Others have been abducted by armed Islamist groups in support of the current regime. The first cases of disappearance - of Islamist militants - were recorded just after the January 1992 putsch. The practice continued to grow, reaching appalling peaks between 1995 and 1996, when thousands of cases of missing persons were reported. At the start of the armed conflict, the leaders in Algiers tried to deny the existence of such practices, or to play them down by referring to "isolated cases" or by claiming that they concerned Islamist militants who had joined the armed groups or had been kidnapped by them.

Most of the missing persons were abducted by security forces in the middle of the night. However, cases of disappearance have been reported following arrests made during the day, either at workplaces or near university centers, or sometimes in the street. The age group most affected is the twenty-three-year-olds, but kidnappings of teenagers and the elderly have also been reported. According to the association Algéria-Watch, the age of the abductees ranges from 14 to 79. The intellectual level of these people is acceptable, far from the theories conveyed by the press close to the government or by some of its mouthpieces, making them out to be scum, beggars or ignoramuses: thus, we find executives, doctors, academics, journalists, company directors, shopkeepers, students...

The security services often used unmarked cars, fake police cards and license plates, and the kidnappers were often disguised and made-up, wearing fake moustaches and beards. They would arrive by breaking down doors, weapons drawn, never to be identified. Under Algerian law, a suspect may remain in police custody for 48 hours, after which time he or she must be presented to the Public Prosecutor by the judicial police officer. This period can extend to twelve days in the case of crimes classified as terrorist or subversive acts, without the possibility of seeing a lawyer, which is contrary to international law. Theoretically, the latter allows a detainee to benefit from a medical visit or to communicate with his family. But the reality is quite different: detainees suspected of belonging to an armed Islamist group or one of its support networks, suspected of being members of a terrorist's family, or of being active militants, were arrested, held in often secret locations, tortured, and once the information they were seeking had been obtained, executed and buried in mass graves. The duration of detention could vary from a few days to several years. The families, often powerless in such situations, received no information from the torturers; they were confronted with a wall of silence, if not threatened. Sometimes, they managed to locate their loved ones, at first, when they had been taken to the torturers' premises, before being tortured and disappearing. Information often came from people who had been arrested for various offences and then released.

The Generals in Algiers, who had turned a deaf ear for years, finally recognized the evidence in the face of the sheer scale of the phenomenon, and the multiple testimonies of victims' relatives, army defectors and various national and international associations. However, although the number of disappearances has fallen sharply in the last three years, they still persist. In its January 8, 2003 edition, the newspaper *Le Monde* revealed that a certain Kamel Boudahri, arrested on November 13, 2002 in Mostaganem by the security services, was missing. The law is still not respected: suspects arrested by the security services have no rights until the DRS decides to hand them over to the courts. Missing persons remain unaccounted for. According to Tigha Abdelkader, there are no missing persons because all were executed by the DRS and buried in mass graves. He estimates the number of executions at the Blida CTRI (Centre Territorial de Recherche et d'Investigation) alone at 4,000 between 1993 and 1997, and there are six CTRIs in Algeria. As early as 1998, mass graves were discovered, particularly in regions torn apart by violence (Larbaa in the Mitidja, Relizane in the west...). Part of the so-called private press, close to the government, declared, thanks to authorized DRS sources, that these corpses were those of victims kidnapped by armed Islamist groups. But no serious study was carried out to identify the bodies. Often piled up in wells in an advanced state of decomposition, they are recovered in a makeshift manner by Civil Protection personnel. No appropriate techniques were used. The authorities have not called on forensic anthropologists or DNA extraction techniques, due to a lack of will and resources.

The families of the disappeared, initially on their own in their quest for the truth, became united and organized in associations, supported by national and international human rights organizations and opposition politicians. Regular demonstrations were held in Algiers and other provincial towns, demanding justice and truth, but to no avail. Some parents have been threatened, others arrested or beaten by the security services. Their grievances remain in vain; they can do nothing against the power of the Generals, the raison d'Etat and the balance of power at the top. True to their traditions, the Generals in power try to avoid being called to account for their practices, and find a way to close the file. Compensation for the families of the disappeared is one of the means the junta intends to use to buy the silence of those who may one day send them to The Hague. As for the families, all they want is to know the truth, so that they can mourn: "What's distressing is that we don't know whether he's dead or alive." Or: "Let them tell me where my son is buried, so I can go and cry on his grave."

In September 2003, Bouteflika set up a committee to settle the issue of the "disappeared" once and for all. In September 2005, under the Charter for National Reconciliation, he proposed compensation and a declaration of death for all cases of the "disappeared". Some families have already refused.

Massacres of civilians

Between 1996 and 1998, in addition to the bombs exploding on every street corner, the massacres of defenseless civilians and the atrocity of the crimes committed aroused the wrath of NGOs and alarm throughout the world. The places targeted were former FIS strongholds from 1989-1992, mostly located in the Mitidja region. The massacres in Bentalha, Raïs, Beni Messous, Sidi Hamed and Relizane, which claimed over a thousand victims, were the most terrible. They were mostly perpetrated with knives, and very rarely indiscriminately, as the decision-makers in Algiers would have us believe: analysis of these massacres allows us to state that there was a selection of targets and victims (the terrorists may have had a list of families to execute) and that events followed a rational course.

Let's look back at four of the massacres, reported by various witnesses.

In Raïs, first of all. It's a village of three thousand inhabitants forty kilometers southeast of Algiers, built around an agricultural estate and secured by a gendarmerie post at the entrance to the village. During the night of August 28-29, 1996, at 10 p.m., between 100 and 200 terrorists entered the village. After more than four hours of carnage, the terrorists left nothing but horror in their wake: the death toll was over two hundred and fifty. The day after the tragedy, the survivors couldn't understand why no help had been forthcoming, why the gendarmes and community guards who were a hundred meters from the scene hadn't intervened to protect them from the horde, or why they themselves hadn't suffered reprisals. How can we explain this laissez-faire attitude in a highly secure region with highly sophisticated military resources?

Similarly, in Bentalha, a massacre took place shortly after the one in Raïs. This is a housing estate on the eastern outskirts of Baraki, in the eastern suburbs of Algiers. This area, like Raïs, is one of the most militarized in the region. At the time, there were at least six police, gendarmerie and army checkpoints between Baraki and El-Harrach, on the south side. On the north side, a few hundred metres away, there was a military barracks, in addition to those within a fifty-kilometre radius, and Boufarik military airport. What's more, the context, with the Raïs massacre a few days before, meant that security measures had to be stepped up. On September 22, 1996, at around 11 p.m., a group of terrorists numbering between 100 and 200 men burst into the housing estate. Same procedure, same carnage. Four hours later, they left behind four hundred and fifty dead. The day after the massacre, stupefaction could be seen on the faces of all Algerians, who once again failed to understand how so many citizens could have their throats slit in the suburbs of the capital, without the help of the security forces. In the wake of the massacre, voices were raised from all corners of the globe calling for an investigation. But Liamine Zeroual was aware of his fragility in the face of a situation imposed on him by his latest strategic choices; he preferred to back down on some of his positions because of his direct involvement in the conflict as Minister of Defense. Instead of revealing the whole truth about a nauseating war, and despite the pressure of international opinion which could not understand the passivity of the security forces in the face of citizens in mortal danger, Zeroual preferred to invoke non-interference in the country's internal affairs, thus shirking the moral responsibilities of an elected president. He will suffer the consequences of his naivety, which led him to believe in people who never forget, and whose rancor drives them to enlist, if need be, the services of a man like Zitouni.

One year later, in Relizane, on December 31, 1997, in the middle of the month of Ramadan, and just after the breaking of the fast, five hamlets were attacked at the same time by terrorist groups. Five hundred and twenty-nine people fell victim to this attack: 117 dead in Had Chekala, 176 dead in Cherarba, 73 dead in El Abadil, 50 dead in Bentaleb, 113 dead in Oued Sahanne. The army did not intervene until 48 hours later to rescue the survivors. A few days earlier, the army's combined forces had carried out a vast sweep in Relizane, more precisely in Ramka. This area had been taken for granted by AIS troops and served as a supply base for Emir Benaïcha's elements.

Finally, shortly afterwards, lightning struck Sidi Hamed. Sidi Hamed is a village on National Road 29 between Meftah and Larbaa, a former stronghold of the AIS, used as a base for withdrawing and supplying its troops, who were stationed there and replaced by a military unit on October 6, 1997 as part of the truce that later led to the "civil concord" agreements. On January 11, 1998, after the fast had been broken at around 8 p.m., an armed group of around 100 terrorists entered the village and set fire to the massacre of over 140 people. The military unit, stationed at the entrance to the village it was supposed to protect, observed the massacre and did not intervene. The next day, the same word was on the lips of all the villagers: "punishment".

All these massacres, car bombs, the assassination of the monks of Tibhirine, and most of the other events that marked Algerian society during these years can certainly be explained, at least in part, by the three years of stewardship by a general president who wanted to emancipate himself from his mentors.

Zeroual's three years as president

No one thought that in September 1998 Liamine Zeroual would announce his resignation and the organization of early presidential elections. To understand the reasons why he stepped down, as well as all the events that shook the country during his time at El-Mouradia, we need to look back at the itinerary followed by this retired general during his brief term of office, and at some of the decisions he took in the political, economic and structural spheres of the army.

On the political front, Zeroual devoted most of his time between 1993 and 1995 to forging a personality as a man of dialogue. This strategy culminated in his election to the presidency of the Republic. Once in El-Mouradia, he tried to get rid of certain constraints linked to the pre-eminence of the army, by adopting a new Constitution and renewing Parliament. To this end, he chose Benhamouda, head of the UGTA trade union center, to launch a new political formation, whose constituent base was drawn from militiamen armed by the authorities. At the same time, he commissioned Ahmed Ouyahia to promote his brand image as a democrat by organizing a pseudo-conference of national accord on September 14 and 15, 1996, boycotted by most opposition parties. On the following October 14, the government announced the organization of a referendum to revise the Constitution. On November 28, the new Constitution was adopted with 85.81% of the vote.

Some parties protested against this electoral farce, which the FFS described as a constitutional dictatorship. In January 1997, the government again set new electoral deadlines, including the legislative elections on June 5.

The National Transition Council (CNT) adopted the new law on political parties, and in February the law introducing proportional representation. But on January 29, just a few days before the official announcement of the creation of the Rassemblement National Démocratique (RND), the man who was to head the President's party was killed in a terrorist attack in the courtyard of the trade union center in the heart of Algiers, Place du 1er-Mai. His last words, addressed to his friend present at the scene, were: "My brother Kamel, they have betrayed us." Who were they?

The alleged assassin shown on television by the authorities will never take the stand in court to speak. He was executed on the premises of the security forces[97]. Benhamouda knew too much as a civilian to stay alive, and was surely upsetting some politicians' calculations. He was shot for daring to play in the military's backyard without being part of it.

Ahmed Ouyahia, former chief of staff and Prime Minister, replaced Benhamouda as head of the RND. Three months after its creation, this party had a great success in the legislative elections, where it obtained an absolute majority, thanks to large-scale fraud. Some parties demanded a commission of inquiry, but the report was never published.

On the economic front, Liamine Zeroual instructed Ahmed Ouyahia to apply to the letter the agreements reached with the IMF. The latter has pursued a policy of abandoning the public sector, resulting in hundreds of thousands of redundancies. Some sectors were totally liberalized, such as transport, where corruption was the rule in the distribution of the best lines, sometimes with a nominee of one of the decision-makers in control. Even armed groups joined in the feast: they selected the beneficiaries of certain lucrative routes and were paid for the right of way. The others had their buses burned. The same process was used in other sectors, such as foreign trade, where warlords took over imports of pharmaceuticals, coffee and sugar.

---

97. Youcef Zirem, *op. cit.* p. 27.

On December 25, 1995, Algeria signed one of its largest oil and gas exploration and production contracts with BP[98], worth three and a half billion dollars. Other contracts with foreign firms followed: with Total, on January 24, 1996, for nine hundred million dollars; with ARCO, on February 15, 1996, for one and a half billion dollars; with AGIP, with the Canadian company Snc-Lavalin, with Andarko... In all, twenty-four exploration agreements were signed, seven of which led to discoveries. On November 1st, 1996, the Maghreb-Europe gas pipeline was officially inaugurated. It's well known how a foreign company can acquire an investment in a Third World country, especially one under the control of a military junta in the hydrocarbon sector. The ELF affair in France is a case in point.

On the military front, Zeroual tried to introduce changes immediately after his appointment as head of state in 1994, but was soon opposed by decision-makers. In March 1994, a meeting of these high-ranking officials limited Liamine Zeroual's powers and delegated his signature to Mohamed Lamari. A few days later, Zeroual, an old hand in the army, appointed the former head of Military Security, General Mohamed Betchine, as his personal adviser. Betchine tried to clear the way for his friend Zeroual. He was responsible for the successful organization of the presidential elections, which gave legitimacy to Liamine Zeroual. Once elected, he was quick to reclaim the prerogatives granted to him by the

---

98. *Annuaire de l'Afrique du Nord (1996)*, p. 433.

Constitution. In April 1996, as supreme commander of the armed forces, Liamine Zeroual retired some 100 officers, including seven generals[99] (notably Khaled Nezzar, Larbi Belkheir and Hocine Benmaalem).

On June 5, 1996, Zeroual relaunched an offensive against Nezzar's entourage. Seven senior officers very close to him were retired[100]: General Mohamed Ghoneim, Secretary General at the Ministry of Defense; General Abbas Ghozeil, Commander of the Gendarmerie and one of the four generals who had forced Chadli to sign his resignation in his office (he resisted a second time to have someone else appointed in his place, but finally gave in in 1997 and was replaced by Derradji); General Tetaouani, Director of External Services at the Ministry of Defense; Generals Taghrirt and Djouadi, Inspectors General at the Ministry of Defense; Generals Touati and Derradji, former advisors to Khaled Nezzar himself. The aftershocks from these telluric tremors were not long in coming. The Algerian people were the victims of this war at the top. The years 1996, 1997 and 1998 were years of hell for the Algerian people. Liamine Zeroual was forced to resign; his advisor, General Betchine, the architect of his strategy, was torn to shreds by a section of the private press in the hands of the security services: his private life was revealed, and this was a first in Algeria. He resigned as presidential advisor. According to *Maghreb*

---

99. *Ibid.* p. 415.
100. *Ibid*, p. 456.

Confidentiel of November 30, 1995, he was applying for a post as Minister of Defense.

The assassination of singer Lounès Matoub

The Lounès Matoub affair alone shows that those who really hold power in Algeria will stop at nothing. The assassination came at a time when the clan war between generals was in full swing. This umpteenth political assassination is part of a war strategy in which the destabilization of competitors is a game that our leaders have mastered to perfection. This explains the constant temptation to break up a region that has been spared large-scale massacres and least affected by the last ten years of war.

By attributing this despicable crime to Hassan Hattab, leader of the Groupe Salafiste pour la Prédication et le Combat (GSPC), a splinter group of the GIA, those responsible were sending a warning to the other clans and exonerating themselves. As for Lounès Matoub, history will record that in 1988 the GSPC did not exist, and that his life was saved only by a miracle, as the gendarmes chosen to assassinate him did their job: not only did they riddle him with bullets, but they believed they had killed him. This was just a reminder for those who still doubted the assassins.

Despite this precedent, following the interruption of the electoral process, the man chose a side he believed to be his own. In October 1994, in the midst of a school strike (at the time, Zitouni was the leader of the GIA), Lounès Matoub was kidnapped. But thanks to the mobilization of the local population, he was freed after a few days' detention in the maquis, with a message to the Kabyles. The testimony of the singer's sister gives us an insight into what the terrorists who kidnapped him in 1994 expected of him: "That night, several times, he told me that we were wrong about them, that they weren't after the Kabyles but the government, that they were for Tamazight. I was worried. Lounès had been changed. He was unrecognizable."

In June 1998, just after the announcement of his death, spontaneous demonstrations broke out in the streets and villages of Kabyle, where thousands of young people came out to shout their anger, accusing those in power of being behind the assassination, and chanting "Pouvoir assassin" ("Power assassin"). This political maturity displayed by the entire youth movement demonstrates once again that the Kabyle street is not fooled, despite its fierce opposition to the Islamist social project. They know who is killing in this Algeria, despite the attempts at diversion by the authorities and their local relays. So to attribute the death of Lounès Matoub, who was professionally executed, to mere Islamist terrorists is not only to have succeeded in killing him, but also to have defiled his grave.

From truce to "civil concord"

On February 25, 1995, Liamine Zeroual promulgated Ordinance 95-12 on clemency measures for Islamist maquisards, better known as the *rahma* law". This law was created in a somewhat obscure context. The presi-

The False Democratization Process and the Second Algerian War (1989-2007)

dency had distanced itself from the FIS, following the letter found on Cherif Gousmi, the GIA emir shot dead by security forces, which Ali Benhadj, number two in the FIS, had sent him, urging him to continue the jihad. Moreover, in the maquis, the creation of the AIS had shattered the unanimity surrounding the GIA, leading to a war of the emirs, starting in the summer of 1994. Despite this rivalry, the idea of repentance within armed groups was initially inconceivable. The Islamist maquisards, sure of their just cause, could not bring themselves to do so. As a result, the majority of those who activated the disengagement process were low-level elements of the security services infiltrating the armed groups. But by organizing the execution of FIS leaders from the summer of 1995 onwards, Djamel Zitouni provoked a trauma in the ranks of the Islamists, and a hemorrhage within the GIA. This haemorrhage was such that even the creators of this "zombie" could not believe their eyes. Some diehards surrendered to the security services with arms and baggage, while others set up their own groups. This led to widespread warfare between the various factions in the maquis.

It was against this backdrop that General Smaïn Lamari made contact with AIS elements via the IEFE (Instance Exécutive du Front islamique à l'Étranger), which later led to direct talks with Madani Mezrag in the maquis of Jijel. Negotiations and the drafting of the legal framework for the truce took place in a European capital. An agreement in principle was reached on September 23, 1997. The AIS ordered a halt to fighting by the following October 1st. Abdelaziz Bouteflika, successor to Liamine Zeroual, will provide the legal framework for this action.

On July 20, 1999, the so-called "civil concord" law was promulgated. Its articles provided for an exemption from punishment for members of armed groups who laid down their arms and surrendered to the authorities, on condition that they had not committed crimes of bloodshed or rape. But even these will not be prosecuted. This procedure was due to end on January 13, 2000.

Abdelaziz Bouteflika called on the Algerian people to give their opinion in a referendum. On September 16, 1999, he won a plebiscite with 99% of votes cast in favor of "civil concord". On November 1st, most of the Islamist prisoners were released, except for a small number who had already been convicted. What makes this story even worse is that two people prosecuted for the same offence were treated differently. One, arrested in 1992, still had to serve a prison sentence because he had been convicted, while the other, accused of the same offences, returned home without being prosecuted. Faced with the legal imbroglio caused by such a measure, the Presidency issued a press release on Tuesday January 11, referring to an amnesty pardon for the AIS elements. But in reality, all those who decided to lay down their arms benefited from this measure, with the exception of prisoners not organically linked to this structure.

Abdelkader Hachani was the last FIS politician still at large in Algeria. By assassinating him, the eradicators wanted to derail Bouteflika's commitment, backed by a few generals including Atailia, to reach a political agreement with the FIS Islamists. For supporters of the no-holds-barred war against the Islamists, this policy was a way of legitimizing the FIS once again.

Abdelkader Hachani did not recognize himself in the agreement signed by the army with the AIS, and was a fervent advocate of a political settlement to the conflict: "The resolution of the phenomenon of violence will, however, remain dependent on a real political opening that would punctuate a fair and equitable treatment of the various excesses that have taken place on both sides." Abdelkader Hachani, Algeria's most closely watched man, fell victim to GIA bullets on November 22, 1999, while inside a dental surgery in Algiers. The assassination was attributed to a certain Boulemia, but during my stay in Serkadji prison between 1999 and 2000, the elderly Casbah native and his two children, arrested for complicity in this political crime, shouted to anyone who would listen that they were innocent. The three members of this family, as well as the presumed murderer, were subjected to the *"el djezr"* principle inside the prison, according to which no prisoner could speak to them. Hachani was highly esteemed by all former inmates. According to reliable sources, his death was the work of a repentant former emir. The latter now enjoys a large and beautiful apartment in Bab-El-Oued and is authorized to carry weapons. This assassination aroused the anger of Islamist circles, prompting Abassi Madani to send a letter to Benhadjer, Emir of Médéa, inviting him not to give up, and asking him to convince the other emirs to take note of the assassination.

The prolongation of the war, which the eradicators thought they had finally won, surprisingly gave a legal and political framework to the agreements reached with the AIS a few days before the deadline for laying down arms expired, when Bouteflika announced a decree granting an amnesty, after threatening to withdraw from certain circles. However, this decree did not prevent the FIS from splitting into two clans, the supporters and the opponents of this agreement.

As for Abdelkader Hachani, leader of the Algerianist wing of the FIS, who had led the latter to victory in the December 1992 legislative elections, he paid with his life for his attachment to a political settlement of the conflict: "Personally, I don't believe in absolution through amnesty, and it would be very useful to meditate on South Africa's experience in this area". This view was shared by a number of senior Algerian army officers considered by the so-called private press to be close to the reconcilers. Among these was General Rachid Benyelles, who, in an interview with an Algerian daily[101], declared: "This crisis can only be resolved

---

101. *El Watan*, February 15, 2002.

through a political solution that necessarily involves dialogue and consultation between those who truly represent the political currents that run through society". But such a choice directly threatened the real holders of power in Algeria, who did not believe in any political current, but in the power of money.

Bouteflika or eternal recommencement

Abdelaziz Bouteflika was co-opted as President of the Republic in April 1999 with the support of the ruling Generals. A young Minister of Youth and Sport in Ben Bella's government, then irremovable Minister of Foreign Affairs under Boumediene, Bouteflika was dismissed in 1979 by Chadli Bendjeddid. After twenty years in the wilderness, during which he worked as a consultant in the Gulf States, he was approached by General Larbi Belkheir to run for president. Belkheir won the support of the other top brass, including retired General Khaled Nezzar, who had previously called him a "nag on the comeback"[102], and who would later say that "it was Larbi who misled the military establishment". The rest was a formality: the administration was put at his disposal, the heavy media praised him, support committees sprang up on every street corner, and he won the backing of the major Western powers. He won an election in which the six other candidates[103]

---

102. Khaled Nezzar, *Algérie, le sultanat de Bouteflika*, L'Arganier, 2003, p. 29.
103. Sifi, Ait Ahmed, Hamrouche, Khatib, Djaballah and Taleb Ibrahimi.

withdrew from the race to denounce the fraud that was being prepared. The illusion he created at the start of his mandate only concerned those who were unfamiliar with the reality of the Algerian regime. To establish his authority, he surrounded himself with his brother and loyal followers. One of his strongest supporters was Noureddine Zerhouni, Minister of the Interior and former head of the secret services, who was on hand to clear the air. He could also count on the support of General Larbi Belkheir, who acted as a buffer between him and the military establishment. Chakib Khelil, Minister of Energy and friend of the Vice-President of the United States, was another influential member of the presidential clan.

During his term of office, he tried, through the referendum on "civil concord", to give himself a legitimacy that he did not have at the ballot box. He gave a legal framework to the agreements concluded by the army with the AIS, but without putting an end to the violence, as other groups such as the GIA or the Salafist Group for Preaching and Combat (GSPC) have not laid down their arms. The famous limits set by the military had to be respected at all costs: security policy, management of the FIS and Western Sahara issues were all military matters.

Abdelaziz Bouteflika soon found himself a prisoner of his supporters, and his room for manoeuvre was restricted. The famous "concorde nationale", which was supposed to pave the way for a political solution with the Islamist movement, remained a dead letter, and he was accused by the Islamists of the FIS of not keeping his promises. For his part, he will shout to anyone who will listen that he is not half-president, but this assertion will not change reality. He will try to emancipate himself by seeking support abroad (in France and the United States), but this will result in institutional deadlock and empty governance. After a few months' honeymoon, during which he criss-crossed the world to sell the image of a new Algeria, and to lift the diplomatic isolation that had weighed on it for a decade, he was caught up by harsh reality. The legislative and communal elections organized during his first term in office, instead of serving as a transition to the establishment of a genuine democracy, served instead to reappoint the old political seraglio. These elections were won by the former FLN single party with the help of the administration, the vote of the constituted bodies and fraud. They represented a real step backwards, returning Algeria to the pre-October 1988 situation: the Algerian Parliament still serves as a rubber-stamp chamber; on the economic front, reforms remain at a standstill, with privatizations of unprofitable public enterprises attracting little interest. Foreign investors are reluctant because of the countless difficulties encountered (transfer of capital gains, land problems, insecurity, corruption at all levels of management, bureaucracy, etc.). As for the private sector, it remains in its infancy. Few operators venture into productive investment. Fortunes built up in the shadow of the single party and under the umbrella of the army are usually transferred abroad illegally. Others prefer to import finished products, aided by the turpitude of the administration. The absence of a free, modern and transparent financial and banking sector is also an obstacle to economic liberalization. The growth seen in recent years remains dependent on oil revenues and agriculture, but is highly uncertain insofar as neither oil prices nor rainfall are decided by Algiers.

While the state coffers are full, the Algerian people are sinking into poverty. The absence of a social policy, unemployment, the displacement of populations caused by the second Algerian war, natural disasters and inequalities in the redistribution of wealth have all contributed to an increase in the illiteracy rate, with a sharp drop in female schooling, especially in rural areas, and to the deterioration in medical coverage. The few achievements of the 1970s (free schooling and medicine) have not withstood the vicissitudes of time. The deterioration in living conditions (promiscuity and lack of hygiene) and the decline in vaccination campaigns have led to the resurgence of diseases such as the plague, the development of water-borne diseases and various epidemics (typhoid, diphtheria, viral conjunctivitis, etc.).

Apart from the persistence of terrorist violence, Bouteflika's first term in office was marked by the curtailment of the freedoms won at such a high price in October 1988, the virtual disappearance of all political opposition with the banning of political demonstrations, the undermining of press freedom with the state-owned press taking orders and acting as a vehicle for official propaganda, the proliferation of scandalous affairs[104] and, above all, the absence of a clear political project.

All these frustrations are behind a succession of revolt movements across the country. During the first mandate, several wilayas were affected by citizen revolts, when Algerians dared once again to defy the murderous bullets of decision-makers, to loudly proclaim their disgust at the contempt[105] shown towards them, and to oppose the introduction of a new system of indigénat in independent Algeria.

The Kabyle revolt

Kabylia, with its thousand-year-old history, has always been a region of peaceful protest. The notion of tolerance is not an empty word, and civic participation is ancestral. At the dawn of the Algerian revolution, it was the bastion from which the voice of independence would emerge. It produced emblematic figures who left their mark on Algerian history. After independence, it became a kind of mouthpiece for all Algerians, expressing their positions, starting with the rejection of single-party hegemony. Over the years, it has become a battleground for democracy. It had the privilege of being the only one to speak out against Boumediene, under the passive gaze of an international opinion frozen in the East-West vision. The year 1980

---

104. The bankruptcy of Khalifa Bank left behind a $1.5 billion hole, as did the Orascom affair.
105. *"Basta hogra"* ("Stop the contempt").

left an indelible mark on this region: fierce repression by the Algerian state, disinformation and propaganda that portrayed it as a breakaway and treacherous region. Having mourned and healed its wounds, the region has decided to commemorate this event, called the "Berber Spring" by the sons of the Djurdjura, every year. This symbol appeals to all Kabyles and demands recognition of their identity and of a part of Algeria's history. Alas, everything that is legitimate is open to manipulation and breeds greed and opportunism.

On April 18, 2001, on the eve of the "Berber Spring" celebrations, as has been the custom for the past twenty years, tragedy struck. Massinissa Guermah, a young high-school student, was taken to the Beni Douala gendarmerie station in the course of a routine arrest following a simple confrontation between young people and the forces of law and order. After being humiliated, he was shot with a Kalashnikov by a gendarme. The murder of this innocent man set off a firestorm, and the whole of Kabylia was shaken by a rare insurrectionary movement. The young people organized themselves and launched a citizens' movement which led them to draw up a platform of demands known as the "El-Kseur Platform". These demands were quickly denounced by the authorities, who cried manipulation and put into force their famous formula of "the hand of foreigners". The young student who was killed was called a "thug" by the Minister of the Interior himself. A campaign of repression swept across Kabylia, with the death toll rising day by day. Despite this, on June 16, 2001, over a million

The False Democratization Process and the Second Algerian War (1989-2007)

Kabyles took to the streets of Algiers, shouting "Pouvoir assassin" ("Murderous power") and demanding that their demands be met. The authorities turned a deaf ear, before playing the usual game of dividing ranks. But the citizens' movement, backed by the region's two major parties, did not waver, and handed the state an unprecedented defeat in the legislative elections of May 30, 2002.

The peaceful movement was put to the sword by the infernal machine of authoritarian power. Lacking a strategy and, above all, having become a card in the hands of certain manipulators trying to catch their breath thanks to the blood of the Kabyles to satisfy the political desires of their overlords, the movement found itself at an impasse. The lack of openness to other parts of civil society, such as women's associations and trade unions, will not help it to spread to other regions of the country. The notion of horizontality and the absence of modern forms of organization have allowed the birth of self-proclaimed leaders or those appointed by parallel bodies (the famous Taiwan delegates), some of whom will be manipulated. The lack of prioritization and structural rigidity did the rest. The movement eventually suffered a setback in mobilizing a population weary of the worsening economic situation and lack of prospects. The leaders were arrested and prosecuted, then released by the new Prime Minister Ahmed Ouyahia a few months before the presidential elections, with a new offer of dialogue.

Since the start of the uprising, Kabylia has buried over a hundred of its children, but no proper commission of inquiry has been able to establish who was responsible. The Issad commission stopped at the entrance to the manor house. The murderer of young Massinissa was sentenced by a military tribunal to the penalty usually reserved for shoplifting. But Kabylia will always remain a powder keg, as long as contempt, impunity of the security forces, graft, corruption, unemployment and, above all, the absence of freedom and democracy persist.

War at the top - Act I

A few months before the presidential elections, a fierce war broke out between the President and his clan and his former sponsors. Bouteflika, "consensus" candidate according to some, "least bad candidate" according to others (such as General Major Lamari, former Chief of Staff), was no longer unanimously supported in the upper echelons of power. As we saw earlier, as soon as he was elected, Bouteflika tried to emancipate himself from his sponsors, the high-ranking military brass, but in a country where civilian power is no more than a shop window, this is no mean feat, especially when the elections that bring you to the top are tainted by fakery to the point of caricature. Bouteflika, brought up in the culture of the single party and the mystification of the "guide" in the wake of Colonel Boumediene, is out of touch with today's reality. The four years of his first mandate bear witness to this. They were marked by a decline in fundamental freedoms, both individual and collective, by the impoverishment of society and by political procrastination. Reforms in education, the justice system and the civil service, for example, have remained in the middle of the road.

But the anti-Bouteflika slingshot - and here lies the problem - was not led by a structured democratic opposition supported by a dynamic civil society and conveying messages of equality, freedom and tolerance. It was led by former single-party apparatchiks, spurred on underhand by scorched-earth gravediggers. What was suggested, proposed, demanded and then imposed on the Algerian people was not a choice between Bouteflika and a genuinely democratic opposition, but between Bouteflika and Ali Benflis, his former Prime Minister. Indeed, Benflis represents the very type of token apparatchik. An old FLN activist and lawyer by training, Benflis has long connived with Bouteflika, even supporting the latter's reinstatement on the FLN Central Committee a few years ago, from which he had been expelled under Chadli Bendjeddid before being prosecuted by the State Audit Office. Ali Benflis was his campaign manager during the 1999 elections, then his chief of staff and finally his head of government. In January 2003, he was received in Paris as a possible successor to Bouteflika. On March 19, 2003, Benflis was reappointed head of the FLN for a five-year term, with extensive prerogatives. On May 5, 2003, he was dismissed, not because of differences of opinion on political conduct, but because he himself had wanted to emancipate himself from his mentor.

A tragi-comedy is offered daily to the Algerian people, where yesterday's courtiers have become today's worst opponents. A cynical struggle for power, characterized by slander, lies, insults and verbal and physical aggression, has pitted two people who share the same values against each other. Benflis had the support of most of the FLN's 2003 leadership. The other party had already sensed the wind had changed and joined the camp of the "redresseurs", led by Belkhadem, Minister of Foreign Affairs at the time of the elections and recently appointed head of government. This clan struggle against a backdrop of regionalism and tribalism has been the talk of the Algerian press. Part of the so-called private press, hostile to Bouteflika for his supposedly conciliatory stance towards the FIS Islamists, took up the cause of his former Prime Minister.

But don't be fooled: the Algerian public press and audio-visual media are not free. They are controlled by private interest groups whose primary concern is not the salvation of Algeria, and are infiltrated by elements of the secret services. It's a partisan press that echoes messages distilled elsewhere. Unfortunately, the fledgling free private press that emerged in the wake of the tragic events of October 1998 was diluted by the torrent of violence and bloodshed that swept through Algeria during the "red decade". The war between Bouteflika and Benflis was a war between a man and his mirror, between two preachers of the same system. Khaled Nezzar's involvement in this campaign through the publication of the pamphlet "Bouteflika, l'homme et son bilan" is the best proof of the hypocrisy of our leaders. In this pamphlet, he blames Bouteflika for all the evils of the world: he holds him responsible for a resurgence in violence (although security service statistics contradict this assertion), as well as for the Khalifa affair and the hundred-billion-dinar sinkhole[106] left behind. He explains that Bouteflika could only have been aware of this, since his brother Abdelghani was part of the management team. The reality is that Khalifa, the son of a former member of the MALG, bribed numerous people in the upper echelons of power, in the media, and in artistic and sporting circles. The vertiginous rise of this unicellular predates the arrival of Bouteflika. He is a creation of the system for the system. In any self-respecting country, his downfall should have dragged in its wake dozens of high-ranking officials guilty of allowing it to happen out of cowardice and greed. But that's not how things are in Algeria! Bouteflika is also accused of corruption. He is also accused of having acquired a ranch in Dubai, and his brother Saïd of having bought a luxury apartment in Paris. Faced with such serious accusations levelled against the President by one of the decision-maker generals, a judge should take charge of the case, as in any country in the world where governors are democratically elected. But the quest for truth in Algeria remains unreal. It would only make sense in a democratic Algeria, with a representative parliament and an independent judiciary.

---

106. 1.5 billion euros.

And for this to happen, we would also need to update all the commissions of inquiry buried under the altar of raison d'état by successive powers since Bouteflika's arrival: those concerning the events of October 1988, the assassination of Boudiaf, the disappeared, the massacres, the citizens' revolt in Kabylia, the coup d'état of 1992...

In reality, Nezzar is not defending the Republic. The 1992 coup d'état was not a rescue of the Republic, but the perpetuation of a system. The victim was not political Islamism, but the Algerian people. The dissident Islamists of the FIS were in Ghozali's government, while Nezzar was Minister of Defense. They were under Zeroual (Hamas, Nahda) and still are under Bouteflika. Bouteflika is unpredictable, and this scares Nezzar and those he represents: fear of being let down, and above all fear of reliving the same experience as in April 2001, and of not being able to flee on a plane chartered by the authorities; fear of being held to account for the trauma suffered by the Algerian people; fear of the NGOs and the International Criminal Court (ICC).

Clan Wars - Act II

In 2004, Bouteflika was re-elected in the first round with 83.49% of the votes cast, according to official figures. His opponents were quick to react: they spoke of manipulation. Ouyahia, a Prime Minister already accused during the Zeroual era of being a ballot-box stuffing specialist, was the first to be singled out. In 1997, just a few months after its creation, the RND won the elections against the odds. Today, Ouyahia is the party's Secretary General. At the time, the entire political class was unanimous in denouncing the greatest electoral manipulation in independent Algeria. In May 2006, Ouyahia was ousted as Prime Minister. He was replaced by Belkhadem, General Secretary of the FLN. As the majority party in the Assembly, the FLN lobbied Bouteflika to make the change. Bouteflika is Honorary President of the Front de Libération. Among other things, the FLN criticizes Ouyahia for the risk of manipulating the 2007 elections for the benefit of the RND. For some observers, Ouyahia's ousting is simply the next logical step in the process initiated by Bouteflika to emancipate himself from the mute. Ouyahia is considered to be a clerk of state, very close to the head of the security services, General Major Toufik. They belong to the very select clan of Kabyles in Algiers.

The RND is hostile to the proposed revision of the Constitution, as it may allow Bouteflika to run for a lifetime mandate. Among other things, the FLN is proposing to abolish presidential term limits and to introduce a total presidential model, with the Prime Minister receiving his powers exclusively from the President. This would mean that the Assembly would no longer have the right of censure, and we would see a return to the pre-October 1988 situation. For the FLN, constitutional revision would put an end to shadow power. And Ouyahia's opposition can be explained by General Major Lamari's declaration on January 14, 2004, during an informal meeting with journalists: on that day, he declared that any person vested with the prerogatives of President of the Republic wishing to tamper with republican order, call into question political pluralism, attempt a tailor-made constitutional reorganization, or show contempt for society and the people, would find the army standing in front of them.

Given Lamari's hostility to Bouteflika, the latter decided, by presidential decree, to have him replaced as head of the General Staff by General Gaïd Salah, head of the land forces. For some, Lamari's resignation is the result of his colleagues' softness towards Bouteflika, while for others, he has been pushed aside by Bouteflika, having paid for his pre-election arrogance. A small revenge for the man who, in 1979, was barred the road to El-Mouradia by those who finally called on him in 1999[107]. Most specialists on the Algerian question have described Gaïd Salah's appointment as a provisional solution. Bouteflika knows that such an appointment will accelerate the internal demands of young officers in favor of the professionalization[108] of the Grande Muette: it would put into practice officers who want to emancipate themselves from the tutelage of the two clans that have been tearing each other apart since 1962. This movement could be seen as the birth of a third clan, which could provoke an

---

107. In 1979, after Boumediene's death, a group of former assessors assigned to the revolutionary courts in 1969 (including Colonel Hadjeres) blocked Bouteflika's path to the presidency, regarding him as a liberal close to France and the United States.
108. Professionalization is imposed by NATO and Bouteflika.

The False Democratization Process and the Second Algerian War (1989-2007)

internal imbalance in the Algerian army and, above all, call into question the legitimacy of the old clans. A number of new appointments were made in 2005: Malek Nessib was named Commander of the Naval Forces, Malti Abdelghani the new head of the Cherchel Military Academy (which trains all future officers), Laychi Ghrid Commander of the Republican Guard, and Ali Benali Commander of the 5th Military Region.

To consolidate his power and independence from the black cabinet, Bouteflika offered himself a blank cheque by having his national reconciliation project adopted by universal suffrage. It was adopted by 97% on September 29, 2005. A shrewd calculator, Bouteflika negotiated its content with the military, including immunity for those responsible for the Algerian tragedy, a ban on those who dared to question the official version of the tragedy, and above all the fact that the thousands of deportees from the concentration camps, as well as the hundreds of thousands of people brought before the courts on terrorism charges, would be left out in the cold: those who suffered the worst nightmares in the jails of the security services and who were cleared by Algerian justice for lack of charges.

The theory of a deal between El-Mouradia and Tagarrins can only be strengthened: as evidenced by the steps taken for the early repayment of foreign debt to the Paris and London Clubs (which some economists[109] consider

---

109. Analysis by Zeroual's former economic advisor (*La Tribune*, March 22, 2006).

a populist move, while others see it as a good thing from the moment when, in Algeria, there is no longer any long-term development), as well as the reconversion that was accepted by the Russians to change the military debt into a contract for the purchase of equipment to renew Algeria's military arsenal[110].

Bouteflika seems to have everything it takes to serve another term, barring any unforeseen circumstances, such as his state of health. In December 2005, he left more than one medical specialist perplexed. Between the official communiqué from the presidency and the opinion of specialists on his state of health, the wildest rumors kept the entire population on tenterhooks for over a month. Perhaps this explains the military's slight passivity towards him. Bouteflika's death could well resurrect some old demons. According to *Maghreb Confidentiel* of April 20, 2005, the DRS is working on a possible succession to Bouteflika. Among the possible candidates from the army's political wing is Ouyahia.

Only Major General Toufik managed to visit Bouteflika while he was hospitalized in Paris. The delegation of powers over the administration and all the armed forces, granted by decree to General Major Guenaizia, Minister Delegate to the Minister of Defense in June 2005, is no mere coincidence due to the President's agenda. This gives an idea of the agitation that is shaking Algerian politicians. Even the

---

110. According to www.wikipédia.org, Russia is to supply 40 Mig-29 fighters, 28 Sukhoi-30 fighters and 16 Yak-130 trainers, among other aircraft.

Americans are on board. No fewer than three high-ranking officials have visited Algeria in the space of a few months, including Rumsfeld in February 2006, and very recently President Bush's personal security advisor. Algeria has become a privileged partner for the United States. Since the revision of their position vis-à-vis the Generals in 1996, the Americans have taken over almost all of the Algerian desert subsoil (Algerians need a pass to travel to certain places in the south of their own country). This cooperation has intensified since 2001, even in the field of security. During his visit to Algeria, the head of the FBI praised the level of Algerian cooperation in the fight against terrorism. It's hardly surprising, then, that Algeria is now cited as one of the countries through which the notorious CIA flights passed. For the Americans, the instability of a very good partner in terms of hydrocarbons and security is likely to make them revise their strategies. And the arrival of an Islamo-conservative wing in power could pose problems. The movement of senior American officials would suggest that the United States is getting seriously involved.

CONCLUSION

In recounting this period of our history, I have modestly tried to bring to light some of the "unspoken", which is necessary to understand the facts and, above all, to grasp the meaning of the events that followed.

Although most of the facts in the first chapters of this book had been known for a long time, reporting them was of multiple interest: to bear witness to the memory of all those sacrificed on the altar of the struggle for power, to establish an educational appreciation of the real nature of this power and the mechanisms around which it is articulated, to follow in a linear fashion this method of governance and the harmful repercussions that led to this tragedy.

As a young man from the independence generation, I felt it was essential to understand how a revolution as prestigious as ours could, a few decades later, give rise to monsters who made our people pay a price in human lives worthy of a colonial war.

The trauma caused to the Algerian people requires psychotherapy, which can only be achieved by revisiting history. Today's reality lies in the details of Abane Ramdane's death and all the events that have followed since independence, from the coup d'état against the GPRA to the return of the "least bad candidate". The tragedy of the last decade can be explained in terms of the events that have unfolded over time, and the implausible web of blood that covers them.

Even if some people respond as usual with slander and defamation, using their best henchmen to denounce the bad faith shown in their interpretation of events, the reality is there. Algeria is a rich, unspoilt country governed by despots who have led it to ruin. The latest earthquake to hit Boumerdés and Algiers shows the extent of the decay of the State, the bureaucracy and ineptitude of the administrative services, the corruption that has come to affect whole swathes of society, the preferential treatment in the awarding of contracts, the loss of bearings and the frantic race for money, which, if they persisted, would put an end to the courage and solidarity of our fellow citizens. But the worm is in the fruit, and this regime is its symbol.

How can we ever explain this part of history to future generations? For the deaths of three thousand people, the United States has demanded that the nations of the world take responsibility for the phenomenon of terrorism. What, then, should the Algerian people demand in the face of the murder of two hundred thousand citizens, the disappearance of ten thousand others and the exile of five hundred thousand of its best sons, not to mention the victims of October 1988, the Black Spring, the events of 1980, the repression of the 1970s, and the thousands who died as a result of the conflict between the border army and the maquisards of the National Liberation Army?

What should be demanded of this Algerian who, in his daily life, doesn't know where to put himself, and can at best go into exile to go underground, subjected to the daily humiliation of all the world's police forces, while our decision-makers behave like stars in Western capitals, and their offspring attend the best schools in the world, thanks to oil, the wealth of the entire Algerian people? Algeria's salvation lies not in its governors. It lies in the reconciliation of Algerians among themselves, and in the use of all means to put an end to terrorism. There can be no threshold of tolerance allowing a certain balance, a balance that is harmful, deliberately maintained and destructive, because it does not advance. It lies in the establishment of a genuine democracy, with a freely-elected, representative Parliament that draws up a Constitution fit for the new millennium. And to this end, the political arena must be freed from the constraints that weigh on it, starting with the lifting of the state of emergency and the freedom to demonstrate. We need an independent justice system that is not subject to the whims of the ruler, we need the presumption of innocence to be respected, we need the rights of defendants to be respected, we need pre-trial detention to be limited, we need prisons to no longer be overcrowded, and we need magistrates' unions not to be manipulated. For the sacrifice of its children, Algeria deserves a free, plural and dynamic press that is not subservient to or manipulated by the secret services. The heavyweight media (television and radio) must be freed up and opened up to private initiative. The only thing required of them is respect for a code of ethics under an independent regulatory authority, to prevent them from falling into the clutches of gravediggers and pyromaniacs of all kinds. Fundamental individual and collective freedoms must be respected, and torture abolished. The army must disengage from politics and assume its constitutional missions. Algeria's plurality must be affirmed, and its triple identity (Islam, Berberism and Arabism) respected. Tamazight must be made official and the necessary resources deployed. Women's rights must be respected. We must demand educational reform adapted to today's reality: free from ideological constraints, focused on science and technology, open to the world and a vector of tolerance. We must not squander our achievements, starting with the French language. Algeria must be cured of its deepest evil, corruption, by restoring the values lost on the altar of the various powers. To ensure that the various services that are supposed to combat this scourge are incorruptible, they must be given the human resources and salaries they need. The guilty must be severely punished. Above all, please do not return to the hegemony of pre-October 1988, and let the people live in peace. History has already been written in spite of you, your money and your henchmen.

APPENDICES

CHRONOLOGY

November 1st 1954: outbreak of the Algerian revolution for independence.

December 27, 1957: Abane Ramdane is assassinated by elements of the MALG in Morocco.

July 3, 1962: Algerians vote for independence, and the GPRA is installed in Algiers.

July 5, 1962: Algeria becomes independent.

July 27, 1962: the border army, led by Boumediene, declares war on the GPRA. Thousands of moudjahidins are killed in the fighting.

September 20, 1962: the border army wins the war and takes power.

September 15 1963: Ben Bella becomes Algeria's first president.

June 19, 1965: coup d'état by Boumediene, who becomes President of the Republic.

January 3, 1967: Khider Mohamed, one of the historic figures of the revolution, is assassinated by the SM in Madrid.

October 20, 1970: Krim Belkacem, the main negotiator of the Evian agreements, is assassinated by the SM in Germany.

February 21, 1971: nationalization of hydrocarbons.

December 10 1976: Boumediene is re-elected President of the Republic.

December 27 1978: Boumediene succumbs to a long illness.

February 1979: Chadli Bendjeddid becomes President of the Republic, having been chosen by military dignitaries a month earlier to succeed Boumediene.

April 1980: uprising in Kabylia for recognition of Amazigh identity, dubbed the "Berber Spring" by its initiators.

November 17 1982: start of the first armed Islamist insurrection in Algeria, known as the "Bouyali affair" after its initiator.

April 23, 1985: first social uprising in Algiers, lasting four days.

November 8, 1986: citizens' revolt in eastern Algeria.

April 7 1987: Ali Mecili murdered by Algerian security forces in Paris.

October 5 1988: nationwide popular revolt, bloodily suppressed by Nezzar and his army. The toll: over five hundred dead and thousands of citizens injured and tortured. The youngest victim was six years old.

February 23 1989: adoption of the new Constitution.

March 10 1989: announcement of the creation of the Islamic Salvation Front.

July 1989: General Nezzar is promoted Chief of Staff to replace General Belhouchet.

September 1989: General Zeroual leaves the army following a dispute with General Nezzar.

June 12, 1990: the FIS sweeps over eight hundred communes with more than four million voters in Algeria's first multi-party elections.

June 25 1990: Nezzar is appointed Minister of Defense.

December 1990: Nezzar and his advisors draw up a political plan for the army.

May 25 1991: start of the FIS unlimited general strike.

Night of June 2 to 3, 1991: Mouloud Hamrouche was dismissed as head of government, and the security forces used firearms against FIS militants to reinvade the public squares they had occupied.

June 5, 1991: Sid Ahmed Ghozali is appointed Prime Minister.

June 29, 1991: Ali Benhadj, number two of the FIS, is arrested.

June 30, 1991: Abassi Madani, president of the FIS, is arrested in his turn.

July 25 and 26, 1991: the FIS holds a congress in Batna and appoints Abdelkader Hachani president of the provisional bureau.

October 13, 1991: the Assembly adopts a new division and a new electoral law.

November 29, 1991: the Guemmar border post is attacked by an armed group. Nezzar accuses the FIS of being behind the attack.

December 26, 1991: FIS wins the legislative elections by a large margin, with 188 seats in the first round. Interior Minister General Larbi Belkheir and head of government Sid Ahmed Ghozali declared that the elections had not been marred by irregularities.

December 27, 1991: Nezzar set up a black cabinet to halt the electoral process.

January 2, 1992: the FFS organized a march in Algiers under the slogan "Neither police state, nor fundamentalist state" to encourage abstainers to vote in the second round.

January 9 1992: the coup d'état process is set in motion by General Nezzar.

January 11 1992: President Chadli Bendjeddid is forced to resign.

January 14, 1992: creation of the five-member High State Committee: Ali Kafi, Khaled Nezzar, Ali Haroun, Tidjani Haddam and Mohamed Boudiaf (appointed Chairman).

January 16, 1992: Boudiaf returns to Algeria. On the same day, the first meeting to unify the armed groups was held in the Zbarbar mountains. Zebda, Sahnouni, Chebouti, Meliani and Mekhloufi took part.

January 22 1992: arrest of Abdelkader Hachani, FIS number 3.

February 6, 1992: an attack on a police patrol in the Casbah district of Algiers leaves six people dead. The machine gun used by the armed group belonged to the Admiralty barracks in Algiers.

February 9, 1992: a state of emergency is declared.

February 13, 1992: announcement of the creation of seven deportation camps in the middle of the Algerian desert (Reggane, Aïn Salah, Ouargla, Borj Omar Idriss, Menea, Oued Namous, and Aïn M'Guel, which only closed in November 1995). Some of these camps were located in areas where the French army had carried out nuclear, chemical and bacteriological tests (Reggane, Aïn M'Guel, Oued Namous).

March 2, 1992: announcement of the discovery of new oil deposits in southern Algeria.

March 4 1992: dissolution of the FIS.

March 30, 1992: General Mohamed Lamari is dismissed and retired by Boudiaf. On the same day, Nezzar reclaimed him and appointed him advisor to Boudiaf.

April 1992: congress of all the emirs of the armed groups in Zbarbar. It ends with the birth of the MIA. Abdelkader Chebouti is appointed national emir.

April 22, 1992: the CCN is created by the government to fill the vacuum created by the absence of an elected parliament.

May 30, 1992: Algeria launches a campaign to distribute operating permits in the South.

June 29, 1992: Boudiaf is assassinated in Annaba during an official visit.

July 5, 1992: Mohamed Lamari, Djennouhat and several other generals are promoted to the rank of major general.

July 15 1992: FIS leaders Abassi Madani and Ali Benhadj are sentenced by the Blida military court to twelve years' imprisonment each.

July 19 1992: Belaïd Abdeslam forms his new government.

August 26, 1992: deadly attack at Algiers airport.

September 26, 1992: Major General Mohamed Lamari is appointed head of the CCCALAS.

September 30, 1992: promulgation of the Anti-Terrorism Act.

November 30 1992: curfew introduced in central France.

December 30, 1992: French convert Roger Guyon is sentenced to death by the Algiers court for membership of a terrorist group.

January 5, 1993: Layada proclaimed himself commander of the armed groups.

January 8 1993: Roland Dumas visits Algiers.

February 7, 1993: state of emergency renewed.

February 13, 1993: French Finance Minister visits Algiers. France allocates five billion francs in trade credits to Algeria (over the course of 1993, France will provide Algeria with two billion dollars in aid). On the same day, Mohamed Lamari becomes Army Chief of Staff.

February 18, 1993: Belaïd Abdeslam visits Paris.

May 17 1993: announcement of seven death sentences in the Algiers airport bombing trial.

May 26, 1993: attack on writer and intellectual Tahar Djaout, who died on June 2. This was the first in a long series of attacks attributed to Islamists.

June 10 1993: arrest of Layada, GIA emir in Morocco.

June 16, 1993: Reda Malek visits France.

July 5, 1993: Smaïn Lamari promoted to the rank of general.

July 10, 1993: Zeroual replaces Nezzar as head of the Ministry of Defense.

August 22, 1993: assassination of the former head of the SM, Kasdi Merbah, after returning from a trip abroad where he had met exiled FIS leaders. On the same day, Reda Malek was appointed head of government.

August 31, 1993: execution of those sentenced to death in the Algiers airport bombing.

September 1993: birth of the GIA. In the same month, a commission is set up to prepare the national reconciliation conference.

September 14, 1993: creation of the FIS authority abroad.

October 23, 1993: kidnapping of three French consular agents.

November 9, 1993: start of a campaign against Islamist circles in France. Some of the militants are extradited to Burkina Faso.

December 10 1993: General Touati approaches six founding members of the FIS and offers them a dialogue with the government.

January 30, 1994: Zeroual appointed head of state for a three-year term.

February 22, 1994: IMF Managing Director Michel Camdessus visits Algiers.

March 10, 1994: escape of more than 1,200 inmates from Lambèse prison. Most of them were involved in terrorist acts.

March 19, 1994: after a three-day meeting of army executives, General Mohamed Lamari is granted a delegation of signature.

March 26, 1994: General Betchine, former head of the SM during the Chadli Bendjeddid period, is appointed by Zeroual as presidential advisor.

April 13, 1994: Mokdad Sifi is appointed head of government, replacing Reda Malek. Before leaving office, Malek signed an agreement with the Paris Club to reschedule Algeria's foreign debt, which led to a 40% devaluation of the dinar.

May 1994: major reshuffle in the army, affecting almost all regional chiefs.

May 13, 1994: unification of armed Islamist groups under the GIA banner.

May 24, 1994: abolition of provisions on corporate autonomy prohibiting the introduction of private national capital.

June 1994: creation of the first armed militia by the government.

June 18, 1994: assassination of Fathallah, president of the League for Human Rights, affiliated to the government.

June 29, 1994: a bomb explodes during a march organized by the RCD; Saïd Saadi, leader of this party, accuses the political-financial mafia.

July 11, 1994: France announces the release of six billion francs in loans to Algeria.

July 14, 1994: creation of the AIS.

July 15, 1994: the GIA claims responsibility for the kidnapping of two Arab ambassadors.

August 27, 1994: Algeria decides to close its borders with Morocco.

September 25, 1994: Kabyle singer Lounès Matoub is kidnapped by an armed group. He was released a few days later with a message addressed to the Kabyles.

September 26, 1994: Cherif Gousmi, the GIA emir, is shot dead. A few days later, Djamel Zitouni takes his place.

September 29, 1994: "Hasni", the popular Raï singer, was murdered in Oran.

October 31, 1994: Major General Mohamed Lamari is promoted to the rank of Lieutenant General, and Zeroual announces presidential elections before the end of 1995.

November 1st, 1994: a bomb explodes in the Mostaganem cemetery on the occasion of Independence Day; five young scouts are killed.

November 11, 1994: the first report by a Western journalist is broadcast by the BBC. It reveals the torture and summary executions committed by the security forces.

November 13, 1994: massacre at the Berrouaghia prison, killing almost fifty inmates. The bodies were thrown into a mass grave in the vicinity of the prison.

December 1994: experts from a Swiss bank estimated Algerian assets abroad at over thirty-five billion dollars, including seventeen billion in France.

December 15, 1994: another rescheduling agreement is signed with the USA.

December 24, 1994: hijacking of an Air France Airbus in Algiers by a GIA commando. After executing three passengers at Algiers airport, the commando was given permission to take off. On stopping at Marseille airport, the GIGN intervened, freed the passengers and killed the four hijackers.

January 13, 1995: several opposition parties, including the FIS, sign the "Rome Contract", calling for a political solution to the Algerian crisis.

January 30, 1995: explosion of a car bomb in the center of Algiers. More than forty dead and a hundred injured.

February 22, 1995: a massacre was committed by army special forces at the notorious Serkadji prison in Algiers, killing over a hundred inmates.

February 25, 1995: promulgation of Ordinance 95-02 concerning the *"Rahma"* law ("mercy" in Arabic).

March 1995: Algeria reschedules its debt with Italy.

March 22, 1995: end of a major sweep in Aïn Defla, resulting in the elimination of over three hundred Islamists.

April 3, 1995: decree announcing the creation of exclusion zones in southern Algeria, effective May 1st.

June 3, 1995: Boumaarafi, Boudiaf's presumed assassin, is sentenced to death.

July 1995: Djamel Zitouni, emir of the GIA, begins a campaign to purge FIS cadres.

July 11, 1995: assassination of Imam Abdelbaki Sahraoui in Paris.

July 25, 1995: start of a series of attacks in Paris blamed on a GIA commando manipulated by the DRS.

August 20, 1995: Zeroual sets the presidential elections for November 16.

November 1995: announcement of the execution of two FIS leaders, Redjam and Mohamed Saïd, who had joined Zitouni's GIA.

November 16, 1995: Zeroual elected President of the Republic.

December 25, 1995: a contract worth three and a half billion dollars is signed with the oil company BP; this is the first in a long series of twenty-four research contracts signed with foreign oil companies, seven of which have led to discoveries.

December 30 1995: Ahmed Ouyahia replaces Mokdad Sifi as head of government.

January 17 1996: Abdelhamid Mehri is removed from his post as FLN General Secretary.

February 18, 1996: curfew lifted in central Algeria.

March 27 1996: kidnapping of the seven Trappist monks from Tibhirine.

April 1996: some 100 officers, including seven generals, were retired by Zeroual. Among them were Generals Nezzar and Belkheir.

May 23, 1996: announcement of the execution of the Trappist monks.

June 4, 1996: General Saïdi Fodhil, head of the 4th military region and former head of the DCSA, is killed - according to the army's version - in a road accident.

June 5, 1996: seven generals considered to be very close to Nezzar are retired. Among them was General Touati.

August 1st, 1996: assassination of the Bishop of Oran following the explosion of a bomb inside the bishop's residence.

October 14, 1996: Zeroual sets the date for the referendum on the Constitution.

November 1st, 1996: inauguration of the Maghreb-Europe gas pipeline.

November 28, 1996: adoption of the new Constitution.

December 3, 1996: the attack on the Port-Royal RER station in Paris, which killed four people, was blamed on the GIA.

December 23, 1996: suspension of two press titles, *La Nation* and *El Houriya,* known for their stance on the Algerian crisis.

January 1997: the government sets a new election date of June 5.

January 4, 1997: the CNT passed a law legalizing the creation of militias.

January 29, 1997: assassination of Abdelhak Benhamouda, head of the UGTA trade union organization, a few days before the official announcement of the creation of the RND.

February 1997: creation of the RND.

June 5, 1997: the RND takes over Parliament with 155 seats in the legislative elections. Most political parties cried scandal for large-scale fraud.

July 7, 1997: Abdelkader Hachani is released following his conviction on the same day of a sentence already served.

August 28, 1997: Raïs massacre committed by terrorists, killing over two hundred and fifty people.

September 5, 1997: Beni Messous massacre. Over one hundred and fifty dead.

September 23, 1997: Bentalha massacre. Four hundred and fifty civilians killed.

September 30 1997: Marry Robinson declares her concern at the deteriorating situation in Algeria.

October 1, 1997: the unilateral truce announced by the Islamic Salvation Army a week earlier comes into effect.

October 14, 1997: Amnesty International, the International League for Human Rights, Human Rights Watch and Reporters Sans Frontières call for an international commission of inquiry into the massacres in Algeria.

October 23, 1997: RND wins 60% of seats in local elections, where fraud was widespread.

December 31, 1997: five hamlets were attacked at the same time in the wilaya of Relizane by terrorists; five hundred and twenty-nine citizens were murdered.

January 1998: the U.S. Department of Homeland Security calls for an international commission of inquiry.

January 11, 1998: massacre in the village of Sidi Hamed; over one hundred and fifty dead, a hundred of whom were burned alive by terrorists.

January 19, 1998: European Troika delegation visits Algeria.

February 8, 1998: European parliamentary delegation visits Algiers.

June 1998: Assassination of Kabyle singer Lounès Matoub.

July 22, 1998: UN panel visits Algiers.

August 20, 1998: in a speech to the nation to mark Moudjahid Day, Zeroual spoke of a malaise within the State.

September 11, 1998: Zeroual announces the organization of early presidential elections.

October 1998: General Betchine resigns from his post following a press campaign implicating him in several affairs.

December 19 1998: Smaïl Hamdani is appointed head of government, replacing Ahmed Ouyahia.

January 1999: some decision-makers oppose Bouteflika's arrival. The real power pushed back the date of the presidential elections to April.

April 14, 1999: the six candidates running in the presidential election against Bouteflika withdrew, denouncing the decision-makers' bias in favour of Bouteflika and the preparation of widespread fraud.

April 15, 1999: Abdelaziz Bouteflika is elected President, to no one's surprise. Secular political parties such as the RCD, and Islamist parties such as the MSP, gave him their support.

July 20, 1999: the Civil Concord Act is promulgated.

September 16, 1999: in a popular referendum organized by the government, 99% of voters said "yes" to civil concord.

November 1st, 1999: most Islamist prisoners sentenced to short prison terms are released.

November 22, 1999: Abdelkader Hachani, number 3 of the FIS, was assassinated in a dental surgery in the center of Algiers.

January 11, 2000: the Presidency issued a press release speaking of an amnesty pardon for AIS elements, just two days before the expiry of the ultimatum given to them to lay down their arms.

March 29, 2000: the government authorized four NGOs to visit Algiers.

August 26, 2000: Benflis replaces Benbitour as head of government.

September 2000: General Belkheir is appointed presidential advisor.

April 18, 2001: young high-school student Guermah Massinissa is murdered on the premises of the gendarmerie in Béni Douala, marking the start of a popular revolt in Kabylia.

April 25, 2001: three complainants (Lyes Laribi, Boukezouha and Si Mozrag) file a torture complaint against General Nezzar with the Paris public prosecutor's office, taking advantage of his presence on French soil. That same evening, with the help of the French authorities, he was exfiltrated in a special plane dispatched from Algiers.

May 2001: the names of the plaintiffs were quoted by an Algerian daily newspaper, which attributed the information to a French judicial source.

June 16, 2001: over one and a half million Kabyles demonstrate in Algiers. Manipulation by the security forces caused the peaceful march to degenerate into a confrontation between citizens.

July 27, 2001: in a preliminary report, the head of the commission of inquiry, Professor Issad Mohamed, accuses the security forces of having used their weapons of war against the demonstrators.

November 10, 2001: flooding in Bab-El-Oued, killing more than 800 people in a few hours. The military authorities were accused of concreting over the large water drainage pipes between Bouzaréah and Qaa Essour during their anti-terrorist campaign.

December 2001: in a final report, the commission of inquiry deplores the fact that it was unable to continue its work due to a lack of access to information.

April 4, 2002: General Nezzar is questioned at his own request by the Paris Criminal Brigade, following the complaint lodged against him in April 2001.

April 22, 2002: signing of the association agreement between the European Union and Algeria.

May 30, 2002: legislative elections won by the FLN, with an abstention rate (54%) unprecedented in Algeria's history.

June 28, 2002: new complaints were again lodged against General Nezzar, including one by Lyes Laribi, who published the book *Dans les geôles de Nezzar* (Paris-Méditerranée) on the same day.

July 1st, 2002: General Nezzar's libel suit against Second-Lieutenant Souaïdia begins. After five days of debate, the general's case was dismissed in September.

July 21, 2002: start of a series of citizens' revolts in the Algérois region, denouncing the mismanagement of town halls.

July 22, 2002: General Nezzar attacks President Bouteflika in the press.

October 2002: local and departmental elections won by the FLN.

October 5, 2002: start of arrests of delegates from Kabylia's *archs* (village committees).

October 30, 2002: Boualem Bensaïd is sentenced to life imprisonment for three attacks committed in Paris in 1995.

November 13, 2002: student B. Kamel was arrested by members of the security forces in Relizane. Since then, he has been missing; his family speaks of an extrajudicial execution.

January 17, 2003: Benflis received in Paris as a possible successor.

March 19, 2003: Benflis is reappointed head of the FLN for a five-year term, with significant prerogatives.

May 5, 2003: Benflis dismissed, Ouyahia replaces him as head of government.

June 27, 2003: FLN announces Benflis' candidacy.

October 16, 2003: Salah Eddine Sidhoum acquitted by Algiers court.

December 8, 2003: death of Sheikh Sahnoun, the last of the wise ulama.

January 14, 2004: General Major Lamari invites journalists to an informal meeting; on the same day, the editor of the newspaper *Le Matin* is sentenced to two years in prison.

March 16, 2004: the GSPC's number two, Abderazak El Para, is captured in Chad; within a few days, the Algerians discover in Nezzar's former bodyguard a troublesome man that no state wants alive.

April 8, 2004: Bouteflika is re-elected with 83.49% of the vote.

July 2004: General Major Gaid Salah, commander of the ground forces, replaces General Major Mohamed Lamari as head of the General Staff.

September 2004: major reshuffle in the military hierarchy.

May 2005: Ksentini declares that 500,000 people have been brought before the courts on terrorism charges.

May and June 2005: a new reshuffle in the military hierarchy, and Guenaizia obtained delegation of powers over the administration and all the armed forces by presidential decree.

July 2005: Bouteflika backs down on the appointment of Bachir Tartag as head of the DCE to replace Smaïn Lamari.

September 29, 2005: the Charter for National Reconciliation is adopted by 97%.

November 25, 2005: Bouteflika is hospitalized in Val-de-Grâce for a hemorrhagic ulcer.

December 15, 2005: Bernard Debré, a specialist in urology, declares that Bouteflika is likely to be suffering from stomach cancer.

December 31, 2005: Bouteflika returns to Algiers.

February 2006: Rumsfeld visits Algiers.

March 2006: Putin visits Algiers and signs an agreement committing Russia to supplying Algeria with its best military technology.

April 2006: rumors circulate that the DRS is preparing Bouteflika's succession.

May 5, 2006: Ouyahia is dismissed and replaced by Belkhadem as head of government.

June 2006: the FLN (National Liberation Front) proposed a highly controversial revision of the Constitution to the President.

ACRONYMS

AIS: Islamic Salvation Army

ALN: Armée de Libération Nationale (National Liberation Army)

ANP: People's National Army

APN: Assemblée Populaire Nationale (National People's Assembly)

IBRD: International Bank for Research and Development

BMPJ: Brigade Mobile de la Police Judiciaire (Mobile Judicial Police Brigade)

BSS: Bureau des Services de Sécurité

CCCALAS: Centre de Conduite et de Coordination des Actions de Lutte Anti-Subversive (Center for the Conduct and Coordination of Anti-Subversive Actions)

CCE: Coordination and Execution Committee

CCN: National Advisory Council

EEC: Committee of European States

CFT: Corps des Forces Terrestres

CIA: Central Intelligence Agency

CNRA: Conseil National de la Révolution Algérienne (National Council of the Algerian Revolution)

CNSA: Comité National pour la Sauvegarde de l'Algérie (National Committee for the Safeguard of Algeria)

CNT: Conseil National de Transition (National Transition Council)

CTRI: Centre Territorial de Recherche et d'Investigation (Territorial Research and Investigation Center)

DCE : Direction du Contre-Espionnage

DCSA: Direction de Contrôle de la Sécurité de l'Armée (Army Security Control Department)

DGPS: Délégation Générale de la Prévention et de la Sécurité (General Delegation for Prevention and Safety)

DRS: Direction du Renseignement et de la Surveillance (Intelligence and Surveillance Directorate)

DST: Direction de la Sûreté du Territoire (Department of Territorial Security)

FAF: Algerian Brotherhood in France

FBI: Federal Bureau of Investigation

FFS: Front des Forces Socialistes (Socialist Forces Front)

FIS: Islamic Salvation Front

FLN: National Liberation Front

IMF: International Monetary Fund

GIA: Armed Islamic Group

GIGN: Groupe d'Intervention de la Gendarmerie Nationale (National Gendarmerie Intervention Group)

GIS: Groupe d'Intervention Spéciale (Special Intervention Group)

GPRA: Provisional Government of the Algerian Republic

GSPC: Salafist Group for Preaching and Combat

HCE: High State Committee

HCS: High Security Council

KGB: Komitet Gossoudarstvennoï Bezopasnosti: State Security Committee

MAJD: Mouvement Algérien de la Jeunesse Démocratique (Algerian Democratic Youth Movement)

MALG: Ministry of Armament and General Liaison

MAOL: Mouvement Algérien des Officiers Libres (Algerian Free Officers Movement)

MDA: Movement for Democracy in Algeria

MDRA: Mouvement Démocratique Républicain Algérien (Algerian Democratic Republican Movement)

IEM: Islamic State Movement

MIA: Armed Islamic Movement

MNR: National Renewal Movement

MSP: Mouvement de la Société pour la Paix (Movement of Society for Peace)

MTLD: Movement for the Triumph of Democratic Freedoms

OAS: Secret Army Organization

OJAL: Organization of Free Algerian Youth

NGO: Non-Governmental Organization

UN: United Nations

PAGS: Socialist Avant-Garde Party

PPA: Algerian People's Party
PRA: Algerian Renewal Party
PRS: Socialist Revolution Party
PT: Workers' Party
RCD: Rally for Culture and Democracy
RND: National Democratic Rally
SM: Military Security
ICTY: International Criminal Tribunal
UDMA: Democratic Union of the Algerian Manifesto
UGTA: General Union of Algerian Workers
UNEA: National Union of Algerian Students

APPOINTMENTS OF ALGERIAN GENERALS SINCE 1964

The 7th military region (RM) was incorporated into the 1st region in 1984; the last region chief was Ali Bouhadja, while the first was Mohand Oulhadj.

1re RM: the first military region covers the capital and the center; its headquarters are in Blida.

2nd RM: the second military region covers the whole of the West; its headquarters are in Oran.

3rd RM: the third military region covers the entire southwest; its headquarters are in Bechar.

4th RM: the fourth military region covers the entire southeast; its headquarters are in Ouargla.

5e RM: the fifth military region covers the whole of the east of France, with its headquarters in Constantine.

6th RM: the sixth military region covers the whole of the far south; its headquarters are in Tamenrasset.

1st military region:
1964-1967: Saïd Abid
1967-1979: Belhouchet
1979-1988: Atailia
1988-1994: Djenouhat
1994-1997: Saïd Bey
1997-2000: Boughaba
2000-2004: Fodhil Cherif
Since 2004: Habib Chentouf

2nd military region:
1964-1979: Chadli Bendjeddid
1979-1984: Kamel Abderahim
1984-1987: Benmaalem
1987-1992: Khelifa Rahim
1992-1994: Gaid Salah
1994-1996: Bekkouche
1996-1997: Kamel Abderahmane
1997-1999: Baaziz
1999-2004: Kamel Abderahmane
Since 2004: Saïd Bey

3rd military region:
1964-1965: Colonel Sufi
1965-1967: Yahiaoui
1969-1975: Zerguini
1975-1979: Salim Saadi
1979-1982: Nezzar

1982-1983: Hachichi
1983-June 1987: Zeroual
June 1987-Dec. 1987: Betchine
Dec. 1987-1992: Derradji
1992-1994: Boughaba
1994-1997: Benhadid
1997-2000: Guedaidia
2000-2004: Tafer
Since 2004: Cheningniha

4th military region:
1964-1965: Amar Mellah
1965-1967: Abdelghani
1967-1969: Zerguini
1969-1979: Atailia
1979-1984: Benmaalem
1984-1987: Betchine
1987-1988: Benmaalem
1988-1990: Gheniem
1990-1992: Djouadi
1992-1994: Bekkouche
1994-1996: Saïdi Fodhil
1996-1997: Saheb Abdelmajid
1997-1999: Kamel Abderahmane
1999-2005: Saheb Abdelmajid
Since 2005: Abderazak Cherif

5th military region:

1964-1967: Belhouchet
1967-1974: Abdelghani
1974-1982: Hadjeress
1982-1984: Nezzar
1984-1987: Sadek Reffas
1987-1988: Zeroual
1988-Dec. 1990: Lamari
1990-1992: Boughaba
1992-1994: Djouadi
1994-1997: Boughaba
1997-2000: Djemai
2000-2004: Saïd Bey
2004-2005: Kamel Abderahmane
Since 2005: Benali

6th military region:
1982-1983: Zeroual
1983-1987: Abid
1987-1988: Djenouhat
1988-1990: Djouadi
1990-2000: Kadri
2000-2005: Benali
Since 2005: Athmania

Chief of Staff:
1964-1967: Zbiri
1967-1978: Boumedienne
1978-1984: Chadli

1984-1986: Beloucif
1986-1989: Belhouchet
1989-1990: Nezzar
1990-1993: Guenaizia
1993-2004: Lamari
Since 2004: Gaid Salah

Gendarmerie Command:
1964-1977: Bencherif
1977-1983: Cheloufi
1983-1988: Hachichi
1988-1997: Ghezeil
1997-Feb. 2000: Derradji
Since Feb. 2000: Boustila

Secretary General of the Ministry of National Defense:
1964-1971: Chabou
1971-1980: Latreche
1980-1984: Beloucif
1984-1986: Benyelles
1986-1990: Cheloufi
1990-Sept. 2000: Gheniem
Sept. 2000-2004: Senhadji Ahmed (interim)
Since 2004: Senhadji Ahmed

Direction générale de la Sûreté nationale:
1964-1977: Draia
1977-1987: Khediri

1987-July 1990: Bouzbid
July 1990-June 1991: Lahreche
1991-Nov. 1993: Tolba
May 1994-1995: Ouaddah
Since 1995: Ali Tounsi

TABLE OF CONTENTS

Best sellers Max Milo Editions

Hitler's banker, Jean-François Bouchard

Confessions of a forger, Éric Piedoie Le Tiec

The Koran and the flesh, Ludovic-Mohamed Zahed

Governing by fake news, Jacques Baud

Governing by chaos, Collectif

A political history of food, Paul Ariès

Mad in U.S.A.: The ravages of the "American model",
Michel Desmurget

Mondial soccer club geopolitics, Kévin Veyssière

Putin: Game master?, Jacques Braud

Treatise on the three impostors: Moses, Jesus, Muhammad,
The Spirit of Spinoza

TV Lobotomy, Michel Desmurget